NEFERTITI

QUEEN AND PHARAOH OF EGYPT

NEFERTITI

QUEEN AND PHARAOH OF EGYPT

HER LIFE AND AFTERLIFE

AIDAN DODSON

The American University in Cairo Press

Cairo   New York

First published in 2020 by
The American University in Cairo Press
113 Sharia Kasr el Aini, Cairo, Egypt
One Rockefeller Plaza, New York, NY 10020
www.aucpress.com

Dar el Kutub No. 26215/19
ISBN 978 977 416 990 8

Dar el Kutub Cataloging-in-Publication Data

Dodson, Aidan, 1962—
        Nefertiti, Queen and Pharaoh of Egypt: Her Life and Afterlife / Aidan Dodson.—Cairo: The American
University in Cairo Press, 2020.
                p.   cm.
                ISBN 978 977 416 990 8
                Nefertiti—Queen of Egypt—Active 14th century BC.
                Queens—Egypt
                932

1 2 3 4 5   24 23 22 21 20

Designed by Sally Boylan
Printed in China

To Victoria

CONTENTS

PREFACE

A search of the database of Oxford University's Bodleian Library gives something over a hundred hits for books including the name "Nefertiti" in their title—the earliest being the 1923 publication of images of the queen excavated during the 1912/13 season of German excavations at Tell el-Amarna. This included the first publication of the iconic painted bust that continues to dominate popular perceptions of the queen, and seems thus appropriate as the first stand-alone volume entirely dedicated to her. It was not until another three decades had elapsed that the next appeared, Mary Chubb's *Nefertiti Lived Here* (1954, with a German translation in 1956, followed by a Russian one in 1961), a charming memoir of excavating at Tell el-Amarna in the 1930s. Subsequently, volumes on the queen rapidly rise in number, ranging from works of poetry and fantasy to serious historical studies (some with, probably unintentional, fantastic elements), and an array of other kinds of work in between. In many works, Nefertiti plays a major role alongside her husband Akhenaten or other members of her family, in particular Tutankhamun. Why, then, add yet another book to this already wide-ranging library?

In part, this is because the past few years have revealed new data—or new ways to look at old data—that make even quite recent works obsolescent regarding some aspects of Nefertiti's career. This is especially true regarding its end, where the 2012 discovery of a single graffito showing that she was alive and still functioning as King's Great Wife a year before her husband's death set to naught a range of earlier theories. These new data have, of course, given rise to a whole swath of new ideas and speculations about her and her family. Indeed, the very title of this book indicates the way that the emerging data have fundamentally altered the author's own views on Nefertiti's career: my very first published paper, back in 1981, was an explicit denial of the possibility of her ascent to the status of pharaoh, an idea that I now unreservedly embrace!

Also, by using a format employed for my recent books on Sethy I and Rameses III, the present work aims to present what is hoped to be a fresh holistic view of Nefertiti. This embraces not only what we know (or think we know) about her ancient career, but also her reappearance in human consciousness in modern times, both as a subject of archaeological study and as a much more generalized icon whose true origins have not infrequently become rather lost.

Much of the first half of this book builds on my wider studies of the second half of the Eighteenth Dynasty, *Amarna Sunset*, published in 2009 (with an extensively revised edition in 2018), and *Amarna Sunrise*, which appeared in 2014. The second half draws on a work on the historiography of ancient Egypt that has been in gestation for far too long, and hopefully will see the light of day within the next few years. This second part also owes much to the seminal work on the modern reception of the Amarna Period published by the lamented Dominic Montserrat in 2000, which showed very clearly how the past can be made to serve and validate the present.

As will be seen, a major issue in dealing with Nefertiti and the wider royal family of late Eighteenth Dynasty Egypt is what one does with the results of DNA studies that were published in 2010. These present two distinct issues for the nongeneticist: first, are the results "real" at all? And second—if they are indeed "real"—how authoritative are the genealogical and historical conclusions presented by the studies' authors? Regarding the first, while there is indeed widespread ongoing work on ancient DNA, there are some specialists who would argue that such DNA cannot be recovered in any meaningful way *at all*. Others would argue that the protocols adopted in the studies in question—or the implications of the mummification processes used for at least some of the mummies in question for the survival of DNA—present such problems that the results may (or even must) be the outcome of contamination by modern DNA. As far as the second is concerned, it is quite clear that only "preferred" conclusions were provided in the original publication, rather than the full range of options for the interpretation of the raw DNA data. However, some of the ignored possibilities have now been worked through, indicating that there are significantly different options available for the identification of both the owners of certain human remains and their relationships—all assuming, of course, that the DNA results are, in fact, "real"!

Most such matters of genetics are beyond the ken of a mere Egyptologist, and thus in dealing with them I have had no alternative but to consider what the apparent DNA seems to be telling us, and to produce a scheme not at variance with this. Yet, in view of the doubts lurking in the background, I have tried to ensure throughout that my hypotheses on such matters are moderated by reference to the monumental sources, so that no *fundamental* conclusions rest *solely* on the apparent implications of alleged DNA determinations.

As already noted, recent years have piled yet further historical proposals on the many that had already been put forward by earlier writers. Many of these ideas are mutually exclusive, with even some apparently stand-alone hypotheses actually dependent on wider matters of historical reconstruction. For example, ideas that Meryetaten might have been the mother of Tutankhamun will (on account of the latter's anatomically assessed age at death) only work on the implicit assumption of a number of years' gap between the death of Akhenaten and the accession of Tutankhamun. On this basis, any attempt to present a wholly "balanced," yet readable, account of Nefertiti's career, taking into account the full range of credible opinions, is all but impossible.

Accordingly, this book differs, perforce, from the previous two books in this series, whose narratives reflected, more or less, scholarly consensus on the careers of Sethy I and Rameses III—although there were certain points over which colleagues could raise objections. In the case of the period that embraced the life of Nefertiti, there *is* no such consensus, in which event I have opted to produce an account that is at its core built around my own working hypothesis for the reconstruction of the Amarna Period. On the other hand, I have endeavored to highlight significant areas of dispute in the main text, including more in-depth discussion (where necessary) in endnotes. This cannot, of course, even pretend to be exhaustive, and I am aware that some scholars may think that I have given their ideas less attention than I should; but such issues are inevitable, given the depth and breadth of the matters involved. In addition, some key points, and broader trends in the assessment of Nefertiti and her family, are also covered in chapter 5.

In producing this book, I have of course incurred debts of gratitude to various friends and colleagues for help and the provision of images, in particular Katya Barbash, Nick Brown, Carl Graves, Barry J. Kemp, Donald B. Redford, Paula Terrey, and Athena Van der Perre. For proofreading and comments on the manuscript, I am indebted to Amelia Alexander, Alison Ball, Victoria Baylis-Jones, Reg Clark, Vanessa Foott, and, of course, my wife, Dyan Hilton. As always, however, all remaining errors of grammar and logic remain mine.

ABBREVIATIONS AND CONVENTIONS

AL	Amarna Letter number
Ashmolean	Ashmolean Museum, Oxford, UK
Berlin	Ägyptisches Museum, Berlin, Germany
BM	British Museum, London, UK
Brooklyn	Brooklyn Museum, New York, USA
Cairo	Egyptian Museum, Cairo, Egypt
Kestner	Museum August Kestner, Hannover, Germany
Liverpool	World Museum, National Museums Liverpool, UK
Louvre	Musée du Louvre, Paris, France
MFA	Museum of Fine Arts, Boston, USA
MMA	Metropolitan Museum of Art, New York, USA
Munich	Staatliche Museum Ägyptischer Kunst, Munich, Germany
Ny Carlsberg	Ny Carlsberg Glyptotek, Copenhagen, Denmark
Petrie	Petrie Museum, University College London, UK
RMO	Rijksmuseum van Oedheden, Leiden, Netherlands
San Diego	Museum of Man, San Diego, California, USA
UPMAA	University of Pennsylvania Museum of Archaeology and Anthropology, Philadelphia, USA

A number of protagonists changed their names during their careers. To avoid confusion, the names "Akhenaten" and "Tutankhamun" are, with a few exceptions, used throughout for these individuals, although during their earlier years they were respectively "Amenhotep IV" and "Tutankh(u)aten." On the other hand, and reflecting the continuing lack of unanimity about the identity of Neferneferuaten, she and Nefertiti continue to be distinguished.

INTRODUCTION

During the last half of the fourteenth century BC, Egypt was perhaps at the height of its prosperity. The conquests of Thutmose I and Thutmose III during the previous century had created a network of client states stretching some six hundred kilometers up into Syria, while its Nubian possessions, now constituted as a formal viceroyalty, stretched a similar distance south of Aswan. These were both sources of wealth and prestige, and contributed to Egypt's status as one of the concert of great powers that now maintained a (relatively) peaceful status quo across the Near and Middle Easts.

It was against this background that occurred one of the most striking events of ancient Egyptian history when, seemingly at the whim of one man, one and a half millennia of religious and artistic tradition were cast aside. Often dubbed the "Amarna Revolution"— so called for the modern name of the site which was chosen to host a brand new, if ephemeral, political and religious capital for the country—it lasted for little more than a decade. However, although the forces of reaction were ultimately triumphant, the country was changed, and on many levels was never quite the same again.

Throughout the revolution, its instigator, King Amenhotep IV, later renamed Akhenaten, had at his side his Great Wife, Nefertiti. Since the 1920s, when a painted bust of the queen found at Amarna in 1912, which would soon become one of the great artistic icons of the world, was first revealed to the public, she has become one of the best recognized figures of antiquity. Indeed, reproductions based on that image are now worn around the globe by people who recognize the icon but may have no knowledge of its source. It has taken on a status that transcends its own materiality.

As such, Nefertiti's image has come to overshadow the woman herself, exacerbated by how little we actually know of her with any degree of certainty. On the other hand, her current world dominion presents an interesting contrast with the way in which she was actively written out of history soon after her own death. Dimly and distortedly remembered by only a few later annalists, her very existence was only gradually recognized once again during the nineteenth century AD. Nefertiti's progress beyond being simply a name was initially a slow one, and even then, much of what became "known" about her was often guesswork or misguided extrapolation or misinterpretation from the available material. Significant parts of these early (mis)interpretations have become calcified as "factoids" outside the realm of specialists in the history of the Eighteenth Dynasty. Indeed, the most potentially sensational data that suggested that she had ended life not as a queen, but as a female king, was misread for some eight decades, at the same time creating a wholly illusory sexual narrative for her husband.

This book is thus intended not only to explore what we can reconstruct of the life of Nefertiti, but also to trace the way in which she and her image emerged in the wake of the first tentative decipherment of Egyptian hieroglyphs during the 1820s–1840s, and then took on the world over the next century and beyond. In doing so, it attempts to consider the available data and the options available for creating a coherent narrative.

1 THE CRADLE OF NEFERTITI

Nefertiti was probably born during the reign of Amenhotep III (fig. 2), perhaps around his Year 25 (see page 94). From Nubia, Syria–Palestine, and more remote trading partners poured tribute and traded goods that made the cosmopolitan court of King Amenhotep III probably the most opulent in Egyptian history. The wealth from this financed new building projects throughout the country, including major sanctuaries far into Nubia: here in particular the king could be found not simply as a divine ruler, but also as a god capable of being worshiped by his human alter ego.[1] Not only was Amenhotep III a god at Soleb,[2] but his wife, Tiye (fig. 3), was a goddess at nearby Sedeinga.[3]

In his thirtieth regnal year, the king celebrated his first *ḥb-sd* jubilee. As part of this, Amenhotep's divine essence was further enhanced, the pharaoh emerging as a solar deity possessing a markedly changed iconography, with the now aging king shown as a chubby-cheeked child with almond-shaped eyes, and solar elements prominent in his sporran (fig. 4).[4] This emphasis on solar cults is evident from earlier in the dynasty, in particular with an increasing promotion of the Aten, a manifestation of the long-established Re-Horakhty as embodied in the physical globe of the sun. First found as an independent deity under Thutmose IV, the Aten's status was enhanced during Amenhotep III's reign, a state barge being named "Radiance-of-the-Aten" by Year 11. The same name was bestowed on the king's West Theban palace at Malqata prior to his first jubilee. However, no temples of the Aten were apparently erected, and the traditional gods continued to enjoy full royal patronage. This is seen not only through the foundation and extension of temples, but also the appointment of the crown prince, Thutmose (B), to the clergy of Ptah at Memphis, first as *sem*-priest (the number two in the hierarchy there) and then as the actual high priest.[5]

The appointment of Thutmose to this pontificate was a manifestation of a gradual increase in the profile of royal princes during the first part of the New Kingdom.[6] A millennium earlier, during the Fourth Dynasty, sons and grandsons of the king had

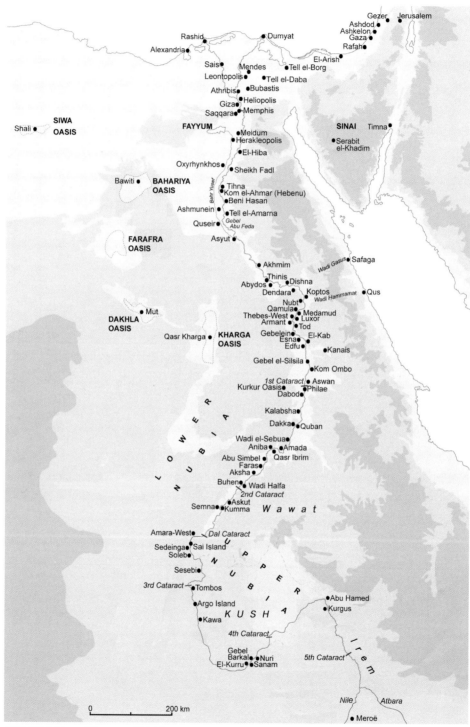

FIGURE 1 Map of Egypt and Nubia.

FIGURE 2 Sphinx of Amenhotep III, from his memorial temple at Kom el-Hetan (St. Petersburg).

FIGURE 3 Queen Tiye, from a faience statuette of her and Amenhotep III (Louvre N2312+E25493).

held some of the highest offices of the state,[7] but under subsequent dynasties they had become all but invisible in the surviving record.[8] Then, during the Eighteenth Dynasty, princes start to reappear by virtue of holding substantive military or sacerdotal positions.[9] This re-emergence of royal princes is paralleled to a somewhat different degree among the royal daughters, who are prominent in Amenhotep III's jubilee reliefs[10] as well as accompanying their parents on statuary.[11] The royal sons are not, however, found in such contexts, and thus a second son, Amenhotep (E), is known only from a seal impression from Amenhotep III's palace complex at Malqata.[12] It was this son who succeeded to the throne as Amenhotep IV, Thutmose having died prematurely, possibly around Year 30, as suggested by a cryptic graffito of that year.[13]

FIGURE 4 Relief of Amenhotep III in the exaggerated "youthful" style of his final decade (Luxor Museum).

A debate as to whether Amenhotep IV succeeded Amenhotep III after a period of corule or only on the latter's death has generated a vast literature, with the battle between the two camps ebbing and flowing over the decades on the basis of the equivocal nature of evidence.[14] However, the weight of evidence currently seems to lie in favor of the view that Amenhotep IV's accession only followed his father's demise. The last known date for Amenhotep III is the Birthday of Osiris (one of the five epagomenal days that followed the three four-month seasons of the Egyptian calendar) in Year 38.[15] Since Amenhotep IV came to the throne somewhere between I *prt* 1 and I *prt* 8,[16] Amenhotep III may have died before the end of his Year 38, although it is not impossible that he could have lived into a Year 39 or even beyond.[17]

In monuments apparently created soon after his accession, Amenhotep IV appears as yet unmarried. Thus, on the lintel of the entrance vestibule of the tomb chapel of Kheruef (TT192) he is accompanied by his mother Tiye (fig. 5b), while in that of

FIGURE 5 a. Amenhotep IV and Maat receiving the homage of the vizier Ramose (TT55). b. Amenhotep IV, accompanied by Tiye, offering to Re-Horakhty in the tomb chapel of Kheruef (TT192).

Ramose (TT55), the king is shown with the goddess Maat as his female companion (fig. 5a). Given that Amenhotep III was previously consistently shown with his wife, while the same is true of his son on almost all his later monuments, it would thus seem that Amenhotep IV was single at his succession, with his mother carrying out the official duties of Great Wife until he married—probably not long afterward.

When the king took a bride, she was a certain Nefertiti, who remained by his side for the rest of his life. It will be suggested later (page 94) that they may have married when the latter was in her mid-teens, soon after puberty. The first record of Nefertiti's existence comes on blocks from a vast new temple complex that was erected at Karnak East by Amenhotep IV, dedicated to the Aten (fig. 6), who is now promoted to a fully fledged god. The buildings comprising this were entirely demolished from the reign of Tutankhamun onward and the blocks dispersed. They were principally taken to form the fillings of Pylons II, IX, and X at Karnak (built by Horemheb),[18] but some were used elsewhere at Karnak,[19] and others strayed to buildings at Luxor and at least as far afield as Medamud.

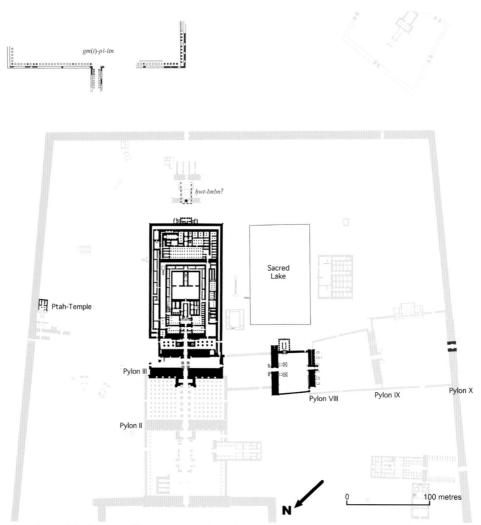

FIGURE 6 Karnak in the time of Nefertiti, with Amenhotep IV's constructions shown in red. Later structures are grayed out.

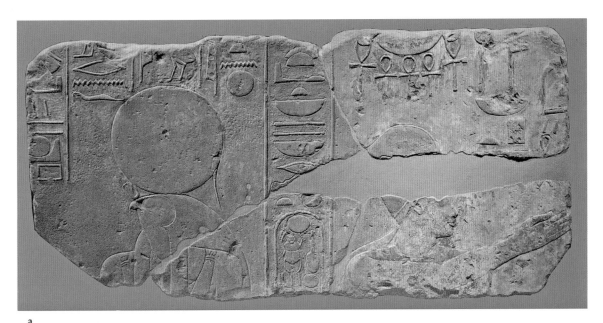

a

b

FIGURE 7 a. Relief showing Amenhotep IV in "classical" style and the Aten in his original raptor-headed form and his didactic name written without cartouches; from Pylon X, Karnak (Berlin ÄM2072). b. Relief showing Amenhotep IV in a transitional style, worshiping the globe form of the Aten; the king's cartouches were later altered to "Akhenaten"; from Pylon X, Karnak (Louvre E13482ter).

a   b

FIGURE 8 The Aten in his raptor-headed form, but his name written in cartouches (a. NMS A.1956.347; b. Aswan).

The earliest phase of the building program included the decoration of the gateway of the just-begun Pylon X, with the Aten shown in the anthropomorphic form typical of Egyptian deities. It borrowed its iconography largely from Re-Horakhty, albeit with a long "didactic" name of a kind hitherto unknown,[20] and the king shown in the "classical" style of Amenhotep III's third decade (fig. 7a).[21] The god's name was, however, soon enclosed in a pair of cartouches (fig. 8), and a little later the mode of depicting the god switched to an abstract form of a sun disk with descending rays (fig. 7b).[22] The latter was at first accompanied by some modest changes in the depicted physique of the king, but this was soon radically changed to what has become known as the "Amarna" or "revolutionary" style, with a lantern jaw and swelling breast, hips, and thighs. It was immediately

FIGURE 9 The faces of Amenhotep IV and Nefertiti as shown in the same scene from the Aten complex at Karnak, with the king shown in the "revolutionary" style, but the queen shown in the "classical" manner.

following the adoption of this style that Nefertiti apparently first appears in the decoration of the temple.[23] Initially, however, the style was not applied to her, there being at least one scene where her husband's features are shown in the new style while hers are rendered in a conventional manner (fig. 9).[24] Nevertheless, the new style soon spread to figures other than those of the king, although transitional depictions are found in the first phase of large-scale decoration of the temple (e.g., fig. 10, and perhaps fig. 118), before the queen joined her husband in being depicted in the most extreme of manners (fig. 11; see further pages 55–58, below).[25]

The blocks used in the new complex were much smaller than customarily used for Egyptian temples, perhaps to aid manual handling and thus speed building, and are

FIGURE 10 Amenhotep IV and Nefertiti, during the jubilee festival; the queen is now shown in a transitional style; from the *gm(t)-p3-'Itn* at Karnak (Munich ÄS4231-7261).

FIGURE 11 Nefertiti in the full "revolutionary" style; from the Aten complex at Karnak (MMA 61.117).

today known as *talatat*, from a term used to describe their size (three handspans) by modern Egyptian workmen. Four separate structures are named on these blocks: the *gm(t)-p3-itn*, the *rwd-mnw-n-itn-r-nḥḥ*, the *tni-mnw*, and the *ḥwt-bnbn*; on the basis of the evolution of style, it is possible that they were decorated in that order.[26] The purposes of the *rwd-mnw* and the *tni-mnw* remain obscure, although the fact that the latter seems to have been largely decorated with domestic scenes might hint at a more residential role. By its name, the *ḥwt-bnbn* would seem clearly an innermost sanctuary, the *bnbn* being the word

FIGURE 13 Nefertiti smiting an enemy, on a block from the Aten complex at Karnak.

for the conical or pyramidal fetish of the sun. It is possible that this was the single obelisk that had been erected on the east side of Karnak by Thutmose IV and would be the center of a temple of Re-Horakhty in the time of Rameses II.[27] This may well have been built on the site of Amenhotep IV's *ḥwt-bnbn*, demolished after his death (see page 97, below).[28]

From the surviving blocks, the *ḥwt-bnbn* may be seen to have had thin walls, fronted by narrow pylons with broken lintels and incorporating at least a dozen square piers, perhaps as an approach colonnade (fig. 12).[29] Interestingly, the king is apparently nowhere to be seen in the *ḥwt-bnbn*—throughout the building, the royal officiant is Nefertiti. This seems unprecedented: previously, the king was always the principal officiant in a temple, and his absence from the innermost sanctuary of his god is remarkable. It is thus an indication that Nefertiti held an exceptional position from very early on in the reign—certainly soon after the birth of the couple's first child, Princess Meryetaten, probably in Year 2. Perhaps even more remarkable is that on other blocks from the Karnak assemblage, Nefertiti is shown smiting an enemy (fig. 13). This icon had been associated with kings since the beginning of Egyptian history, but unheard of for queens,[30] although found many centuries later in Nubia (fig. 14). This is by no means the only case of Nefertiti being so depicted (e.g., fig. 68), with various other iconographic examples of near-kingly status to be found.[31]

FIGURE 12 Reconstruction
of the pylon and colonnade
of the ḥwt-bnbn at Karnak.

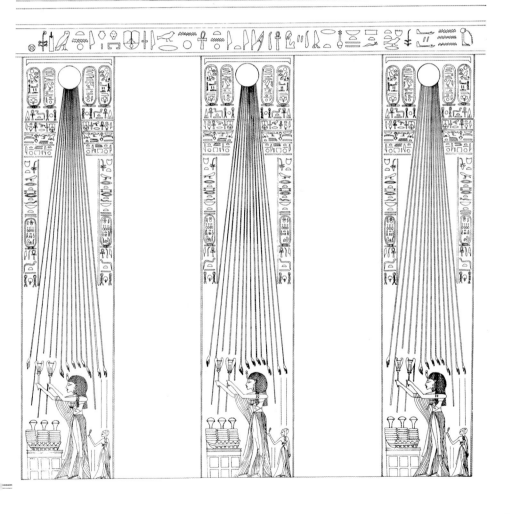

Inner faces

0   2 meters

FIGURE 14 The Lion Temple at Naga, Sudan, with the late first-century BC Meroitic queen Amanishaketo smiting an enemy on the right-hand tower.

Who Was Nefertiti?

The question of the origins of Nefertiti has been a matter for debate since she first became known to scholarship during the nineteenth century (see pages 113–14). Nowhere are her father and mother named on any extant monument—although such a lack of data on parentage is shared by the vast majority of ancient Egyptian queens. Her mother-in-law, Tiye, is in many ways the exception that proves the rule, her father Yuya and mother Tjuiu (fig. 15) being explicitly named in a series of large scarabs issued by her husband, Amenhotep III—a type of commemorative item that is all but unique to his reign.[32]

The only queens whose parentage is secure are generally those who were the blood sisters of their husbands but, even then, it is sometimes unclear whether they were full or half-siblings, as in such cases the mother's name is usually absent. What does seem clear about Nefertiti, however, is that she was *not* the sister of her husband: her exhaustive, frequently quoted titles (page 23, below) lack the telltale *s3t-nsw* (King's Daughter) or *snt-nsw* (King's Sister). Some researchers have employed special pleading to try and

FIGURE 15 The funerary masks of Yuya and Tjuiu; from KV46 (Cairo CG51008–9).

still make Nefertiti Akhenaten's sister, but given the lack of parallels, such a relationship can certainly be ruled out.

One clear fact is that Tey, the wife of General (later King) Ay (fig. 16), was "Nurse of the King's Great Wife Neferneferuaten-Nefertiti." One view has linked this with the meaning of "Nefertiti"— "The Beautiful Female Has Arrived"—to make her a foreign princess, looked after by Tey on her arrival in Egypt, and thus perhaps of tender years. An oft-cited candidate for Nefertiti's original identity is Princess Tadukhepa, daughter of Tushratta, the king of the north Syrian state of Mitanni, who arrived in Egypt as a bride for Amenhotep III prior to his Year 36.[33] From that

FIGURE 16 Ay and Tey, as depicted on the right jamb of Ay's tomb chapel at Amarna.

year comes a letter in cuneiform script, found at Amarna (one of the Amarna Letters—see page 113, below), in which Tushratta greets his daughter as Amenhotep's wife (as he does in other undated letters).

That Tadukhepa subsequently became the wife of Amenhotep IV is also clear, as she is called Tiye's "daughter-in-law" in a letter written to the queen soon after her husband's death,[34] and Amenhotep IV's "wife" in both a contemporary letter[35] and two others which may be a little later in date.[36] However, there is no indication that she was promoted from "diplomatic bride" to Great Wife, especially given the exceptional status displayed by Nefertiti from the outset. While there are plenty of data for the marriage of foreign princesses with Egyptian kings during the New Kingdom, there is very little evidence that such women took Egyptian names and became prominent at court, still less became Great Wives. The one exception is Maathorneferure, the daughter of the Hittite king Hattusili III, who was espoused as a Great Wife by Rameses II in the aftermath of the peace treaty he signed with her father in his Year 21, which brought to an end decades of hostility between the two powers.[37]

Although the case of Maathorneferure is an apparent parallel for Nefertiti potentially being a foreigner, by the time in question the whole family dynamic of the Egyptian royal house had shifted in a major way—and when Maathorneferure arrived in Egypt Rameses already had an extensive family with Egyptian wives. Also taking into account the epoch-making nature of his agreement with the princess's father, King Hattusili III, such an elevation of a foreigner to the highest level of queenship should be seen as very different from a foreigner achieving such a status at the outset of a reign back in the Eighteenth Dynasty.

In addition, the name "Nefertiti" is by no means an unusual one, as is sometimes opined. It was certainly borne by other ladies of the same general period,[38] for example the mother of the Deir el-Medina artisan Huy (TT339), dating to the early Nineteenth Dynasty; at the same site, the wife of Sennedjem (TT1) bore the alternate version, Iyneferti.[39] A further important factor is that a lady named Mutnedjmet[40] is explicitly labeled as Nefertiti's sister in a number of scenes in tomb chapels (fig. 17),[41] and there is no indication whatsoever that she was a foreigner, let alone a Mitannian princess. Thus, there seems no reason to suspect that Nefertiti was not an Egyptian, any more than any other royal wife of nonroyal birth.

So who might Nefertiti's parents have been? The aforementioned Ay is of interest by holding the title "God's Father," a title that goes back to the First Intermediate Period and Middle Kingdom, when it could be used to denote the nonroyal father of a king.[42] In the generation previous to Nefertiti, the title had been borne by Yuya, father of Queen Tiye, and it has been frequently suggested that by the Eighteenth Dynasty it could have taken

FIGURE 17 Mutnedjmet (left) as shown in the tomb chapel of Parennefer at Amarna (TA7); to the right are her eldest three nieces, Meryetaten, Meketaten, and Ankhesenpaaten, each explicitly called the offspring of Nefertiti.

on the extended meaning of "king's father-in-law." On this basis, Ay's use of the title could imply that he held that relationship vis-à-vis Akhenaten—most probably as father of Nefertiti. Against this could be ranged the fact that Ay's wife Tey was *not* "Mother of the King's Great Wife" (as had been Tjuiu, mother of Tiye), but her "Nurse." But could the latter have been used in this case with the meaning of "stepmother"? Indeed, there is evidence that Ay had had at least one wife other than Tey.

It seems clear that Ay had a son, the general Nakhtmin (fig. 18),[43] and a statue of a man with the same name and titles names his mother as the "Chantress of Min, Iuy."[44] Now, while it is not impossible that we are dealing with a homonym of Nakhtmin, son of Ay, the fact that Iuy served the cult of Min is rather suggestive,

FIGURE 18 Head of broken statue of Nakhtmin (Luxor Museum, ex-CG779A).

since Ay was, as king, closely associated with the city of Akhmim, a cult center of that god. Thus, one could hypothesize that Nefertiti's mother could also have been Iuy, who may then have died, leaving Nefertiti to be brought up by Ay's new wife, Tey. Also, tantalizingly, Yuya was also associated with the Min cult, as well as holding the same military

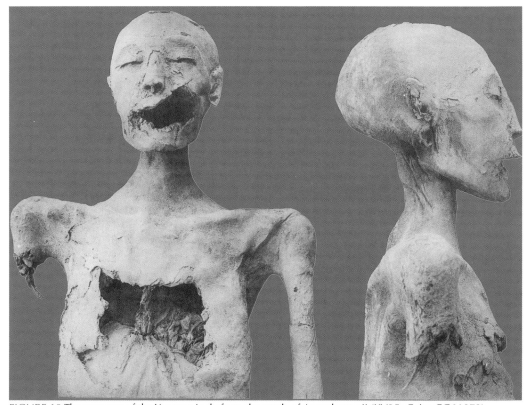

FIGURE 19 The mummy of the Younger Lady from the tomb of Amenhotep II (KV35: Cairo CG61072).

titles as Ay, and a name of very similar form. Thus, the idea that Ay was not only the father of Nefertiti but also a brother of Queen Tiye has not infrequently been mooted by Egyptologists. This would make Nefertiti a first cousin of her husband, neatly tying up various loose ends in the family relationships of the time.

A further strand of evidence was introduced by DNA studies of a number of mummies published in 2010 (see further p. 130, below).[45] In considering this, one needs to keep firmly in mind the methodological concerns noted on page x, above, with some arguing that what has been studied are the outcomes of modern contamination of the ancient remains.[46] In addition, even if the data are indeed "real," it is clear that the conclusions drawn in the publication are very much "preferred" ones, and by no means exhaust the range of possible interpretations of the raw data. In particular, it was concluded that Tutankhamun was the offspring of the individual represented by the mummy from KV55 in the Valley of the Kings (see page 70) and a full-blood sister, represented by the "Younger Lady" found in the tomb of Amenhotep II (KV35—see pages 94, 129–31; figs. 19, 109).

The identity of the KV55 mummy has been problematic since its discovery.[47] Candidates are Akhenaten and his short-lived coruler Smenkhkare (see further pages 69–70 below), but neither has a known sister-wife. As already noted, Nefertiti did not hold any appropriate title, nor did Akhenaten's only other known spouse, Kiya (for whom see pages 50–52, below), while Smenkhkare was the husband of Akhenaten and Nefertiti's eldest daughter, Meryetaten, with no indication that Tutankhamun was also their child (cf. pages x, 140 n50).

Now, while we have many gaps in the list of Egyptian queens, the quantity of material from Akhenaten's reign makes the idea that he might have had a third wife difficult to accept—particularly one whose lineage would have made her a particularly distinguished individual. On the other hand, it has now been pointed out that three generations of first-cousin marriages can produce the same genetic signature in the final generation as a brother-sister union.[48] It should also be pointed out that if the KV55 mummy were a full brother of Tutankhamun's father, rather than his actual father, he would have shared the relevant genetics—and it has often been argued that this was precisely the relationship between Akhenaten and Smenkhkare (see page 70, below).

As already noted, there are good arguments for making Nefertiti a first cousin of her husband, while it has also been proposed that Yuya might have been a brother of Queen Mutemwiya, wife of Thutmose IV and mother of Amenhotep III. Thus, if Nefertiti's mother had been a sister of Amenhotep, the genetic requirements for making her both Tutankhamun's mother and the Younger Lady would have been fulfilled. There is, however, no sign of such a woman anywhere in surviving records, with neither Iuy nor Tey holding the appropriate title of "King's Daughter."

But in this case the "missing woman" would have been a young princess, married to a young army officer, who could easily have given birth to Nefertiti and died—perhaps in childbirth—long before Ay first appears in the records in his tomb chapel at Amarna, constructed at least half a decade after Nefertiti had become queen. On this basis—and here one must repeat the proviso that the DNA results are indeed "real" and not wholly the result of contamination in modern times—a working hypothesis would seem to be that Nefertiti's marriage had been the third (at least) in a series of first-cousin unions between the royal house and a military family from the city of Akhmim. As for which of Ay's three putative wives was the mother of Mutnedjmet, her representations (e.g., fig. 17) may suggest that she was only a little older than Nefertiti's eldest children (although her mode of representation may simply be a matter of the protocols of Egyptian art), which could point to Tey being perhaps her mother. We will return to the question of Nefertiti as Tutankhamun's mother below (pages 47–48), and also to the implication that the mummy of the Younger Lady from KV35 is none other than that of Nefertiti herself (pages 140–41 n.53).

As for the origins of Nefertiti's putative stepmother Tey, it is possible that she was the daughter of an Akhmimi noble named Sennedjem (not to be confused with the aforementioned Deir el-Medina workman). Later a tutor to the young Tutankhamun, his tomb at Awlad Azzaz, near Akhmim,[49] had the title "God's Father" added to its inscriptions after they had been completed, suggesting that, if this indeed meant "king's father-in-law," his daughter had become a queen later in life. The only obvious candidate among known individuals would seem to be Tey.

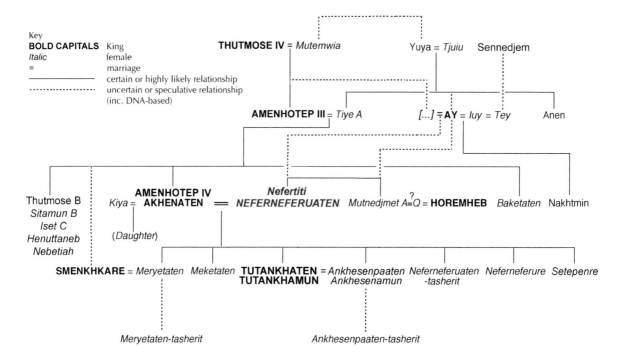

Reconstruction of the royal family tree as proposed in this book.

2 QUEEN OF EGYPT

As queen, Nefertiti used the following substantive titles:

A		*ḥmt-nsw-wrt*	King's Great Wife
B		*ḥmt-nsw-ꜥt*	King's Great Wife
C		*ḥnwt-šmꜣw-tꜣ-mḥw*	Mistress of Upper & Lower Egypt
D		*ḥnwt-tꜣw-nbw*	Mistress of all lands
E		*nbt-tꜣwy*	Lady of the Two Lands
F		*irtt-pꜥt*	Noblewoman

Of them, title A marked her out as the king's senior wife. While *ḥmt-nsw* had been employed as a designation of the queen since the Old Kingdom,[1] the first uses of the elevated *ḥmt-nsw-wrt* version seem to have been during the Second Intermediate Period.[2] In any case, it was in regular use from the end of the Seventeenth Dynasty onward, continuing to be employed down to Arsinoë III under Ptolemy IV. During most reigns only one woman held the title at a time, marking her out as the king's principal partner, although a number of kings (including Amenhotep III, Rameses II, and Rameses III) bestowed the title on more than one woman simultaneously. Nefertiti is the only known holder of the title during her husband's reign. Indeed, the only other known wife, Kiya, held a unique title, *ḥmt-mrrty-ꜥt-n-nsw-bity* (Greatly Beloved Wife of the King), that was perhaps intended to underline Nefertiti's dominant status by leaving her the only actual *ḥmt-nsw*.

FIGURE 20 Relief of the royal family, showing them in a typical tableau of the Amarna Period, worshiping the Aten. Only Princesses Meryetaten and Meketaten are included, dating its carving to around Year 5, when Akhet-Aten was founded; from the Royal Tomb (TA26) at Amarna (Cairo TR10/11/26/4).

Title B is unique to Nefertiti, and even in her case used extremely sparingly, possibly during the latter part of the reign, as it is found in the tomb chapel of Meryre ii (TA2), which contains a scene dated to her husband's Year 12 (see pages 59–61).[3] The significance of the title's use of a different word for "great" is unclear, although its unique nature would tempt one to tie it to Nefertiti's already-noted exceptional status. However, *ḥmt-nsw-ꜥ3t* certainly never superseded *ḥmt-nsw-wrt* as her principal title, the latter being the one given in Nefertiti's latest-known mention as a queen (see page 72, below).

Title C, *ḥnwt-šm3w-t3-nḥw*, seems to have been first used by Ahhotep I, mother of Ahmose I, founder of the Eighteenth Dynasty, then continuing down to Cleopatra VII, the last ancient Egyptian queen. The similar title D was, in contrast, only used from the middle of the Eighteenth Dynasty (Hatshepsut) to the early Nineteenth Dynasty (Nefertiry D, wife of Rameses II).[4] The closely linked *ḥnwt-t3wy* (Mistress of the Two

Lands) seems not to have been used by Nefertiti, although commonly employed from, again, Ahhotep I until the time of Rameses II, and then during the Twenty-fifth and Ptolemaic Dynasties.[5] Like these titles, E (*nbt-t3wy*) references the two halves of Egypt, but also directly mirrors the kingly title *nb-t3wy*, which began to be used early in the Middle Kingdom. However, the queenly version comes into use only with, once again, Ahhotep I.

Nefertiti's final major title, *irtt-p't*, differs from the others in not being specific to kingship. Rather, it is a ranking title, indicating membership of the highest nobility (the *p't*), and going back to the early Old Kingdom in its male form; the female version is found from the late Sixth Dynasty down to Ptolemaic times. It is often translated as "Hereditary Princess" or "Hereditary Noblewoman," but there seems no evidence for the implication that it was necessarily transmitted by blood, and the status could without doubt be simply bestowed by the king. Further confusion has been caused by the fact that from the late Eighteenth Dynasty onward the male version of the title could be used with the meaning of "crown prince," reinforcing now-discredited late nineteenth- and early twentieth-century theories that the right to the throne was transmitted through the female line (see pages 113–14, below).

In addition to these titles, Nefertiti's name was often accompanied by a wide variety of epithets:[6] *bnrt/nḏmt mr(w)t* (sweet of love); *'3t-ršwt* (great of joy); *nbt-ršwt* (lady of joy); *ḫnmt-ršwt* (united with joy); *ḫnmt-nfrw* (united with beauty); *'3t-m-'ḥ* (great in the palace); *i't-ib-n-nsw-m-pr.f* (the one who gladdens the heart of the king in his house); *ḥnwt-ḥmwt-nbw* (mistress of all women); *nbt-im3t* (lady of the *im3t*-scepter); *w'b-'wy* (pure of arms); *ḏdt-ḫt-nbt-ir.tw-n.s* (one for whom her every word is done for her); *ḥry-ḥr-ḏdwt-nbwt* (pleasing with regard to all her words); *wrt-ḥswt* (great of praises); *ḫnmt-ḥswt* (united with praise); *h"ḥ.tw-n-sḏm-ḫrw.s* (one at hearing whose voice one rejoices); *sḥtpt-p3-itn-m-ḫrw-nḏm-m-n3y.s-ḏrty-nw-ḥr-sššwt* (one who satisfies the Aten with a sweet voice and her hands that carry sistra); *wbn-p3-itn-r-rdit-n-st-ḥswt-ḥtp.f-r-q3b-mrwt.s* (one for whom the Aten rises to give her praise and sets to repeat her love); *'nt-šwty* (she who is beautiful in the two feathers). Many of these had been used by earlier queens, but the Aten-referencing ones were of course unique to her, while others were relatively rare; on the other hand, the latter may simply reflect the fact that the number of Nefertiti's surviving monuments greatly exceeds those of most other queens!

During the first years of her husband's reign, these titles accompanied Nefertiti's simple name, written in a cartouche:

      nfrt-iy-ti

However, before Year 5,[7] she began on occasion to use an expanded cartouche:

 *nfr-nfrw-itn nfrt-iy-ti*

This expanded version of her name became the universal way of denoting the queen from around Year 6 onward.[8] Its iconography is odd, with the name of the god Aten reversed at the front of the cartouche, suggesting that the cartouche should be read outward from the *nfr* signs in the center, establishing the two parts as separate names, rather than "Neferneferuaten" being simply an epithet appended to the queen's original name. This is confirmed by rare readings that place the god's name in the center:[9]

This is potentially significant for later developments (page 75, below).

During her period as queen, Nefertiti wore a number of different kinds of headgear—at least seven having been noted.[10] During her earliest years (at Karnak), she is shown generally with the ancient "tripartite" hairstyle (fig. 10), with one image showing the hair in elaborate plaits (figs. 9, 11, 20), or wearing the so-called Nubian wig, a unisex item (for which see figs. 53, 55, 96). The first two are often topped by a modius supporting twin feathers, with (figs. 11, 12, 20) or without (fig. 10) a sun disk and cow horns.[11]

The feather and disk are also found with ram horns atop a flat-topped cap, both at Karnak (fig. 118) and after the move to Amarna (fig. 39). Nefertiti's range of headgear expands following the latter event, with the so-called bag wig employed (fig. 38), along with a simple skullcap of a kind normally worn by kings[12] (figs. 57, 58). Insignia expand beyond the previous feather combinations, including at least one attestation of the *atef*, which is more usually worn by a king (fig. 21; cf. fig. 96). But around the time of the foundation of Amarna a new headdress appears in the record: the flat-topped so-called Nefertiti crown, which is unique to her (figs. 13, 40, 41, 42, 44, 59, 62, 68). It has been suggested that it was adopted to visually (and possibly even conceptually) match the blue crown, which is frequently worn by the king at Amarna.[13]

Jubilee

While work continued on the building and decoration of the Aten complex at Karnak, a *ḥb-sd* jubilee was celebrated and included among the decoration (fig. 22).[14] Its date is unclear, but the fact that none of the fragmentary scenes depicting it include Princess

FIGURE 21 Right jamb of the tomb chapel of Panehsy at Amarna (TA6), showing the royal family worshiping the Aten.

Meryetaten may suggest that it took place early on, as does the fact that the representations of the king and queen are not yet in the fully mature Amarna style (e.g., fig. 10). Although the king is the focus of the rituals, Nefertiti appears not infrequently, both with her husband and playing an individual role.[15]

The jubilee presents a number of problems of interpretation. One is its extremely early date within the reign: the evidence from other *ḥb-sd*s implies that it should usually be held only after three decades of rule, although there are numerous exceptions (albeit none *this* early in a reign). The other is whether it was a jubilee of the king, the Aten

FIGURE 22 Episode from the *ḥb-sd* jubilee as depicted in the *gm(t)-p3-'Itn*, with Nefertiti shown behind her husband in worshiping the Aten (Luxor Museum).

(who henceforth employed the epithet *imy-ḥb-sd* [who is in jubilee]), or even both.[16] One possibility is that it was timed to coincide with what would have been the Fourth Jubilee of Amenhotep III, had he lived: having celebrated them in Year 30, Year 34, and Year 37, the next would have been in Year 40 or 41. Depending on whether Amenhotep III died in Year 38 or 39, this would have corresponded to his son's Year 2 or 3—a reasonable estimate of the date of the jubilee on the basis of the artistic and family evidence.

If it indeed continued the drumbeat of Amenhotep III's jubilees, it would reinforce the suspicion that the Aten was none other than an ultimate hypostasis of Amenhotep III as a solar deity—that the Aten *was* the divine essence of the old king. The old king's First Jubilee had seen Amenhotep III's transformation into a solar deity; this "Fourth Jubilee" will have seen the transformation of the Aten (and Amenhotep III) into the abstract form of the sun disk. Amenhotep IV's participation in the process would then have been as the Aten's representative on earth (soon made concrete in his impending change of nomen), and it may be that the switch of art style was, like that seen with representations of Amenhotep III at his First Jubilee, a reflection of a concomitant change in Amenhotep IV's nature.

The setting for the jubilee seems to have been the great courtyard of the *gm(t)-p3-itn*, whose walls were adorned with scenes of its fulfillment. This is the one part of the Karnak Aten complex whose site has been identified. This courtyard was surrounded by a colonnade, its piers fronted by colossal royal statues in granite, quartzite, and sandstone.[17] The latter were apparently originally carved in traditional style, but subsequently almost entirely recarved in the revolutionary style, reinforcing the idea that the jubilee should be dated very early in the reign.[18] Over sixty statues or fragments thereof survive, perhaps representing some forty to fifty original statues, comprising some of the most striking examples of the distortions of the human body inherent in the revolutionary style.[19] Although the vast majority represented Amenhotep IV, wearing the royal kilt (fig. 23a), some represented Nefertiti. The most intact of the latter was long interpreted as the king naked, but with no sign of his genitalia (fig. 23b).

a   b

FIGURE 23 Colossi from the court of the *gm(t)-p3-'Itn*, the left one representing Amenhotep IV, and the right one probably Nefertiti (Cairo JE49529; JE55938).

This has led to all kinds of discussions as to his potential pathology,[20] but the body is much more easily seen as that of a woman, wearing the usual tightly fitting sheath dress clinging to the upper legs. The piece also has other iconographical peculiarities, in that (unlike those definitely representing Amenhotep IV) its crown—a double crown—sits directly on the head, rather than atop a *nms* or *ḥ3t* headdress.[21] This feature is shared with nine other heads from the corpus, along with the later mutilation of the facial features in all but one case—something not seen in the undoubted Amenhotep IV pieces. One head apparently from the group has double uraei, clearly indicating that it belonged to a queen.

The fact that the statues wore the double crown might at first argue against them being of Nefertiti—but it is now clear that later in the reign she would affect a kingly crown while yet a queen (see pages 71–72, below), and thus it is quite possible that this could have been, on occasion, the case even this early on. Accordingly, it seems likely that a fifth or even a quarter of the colossi in the courtyard of the *gm(t)-p3-itn* represented Nefertiti. As such she may have been present as an incarnation of the moisture goddess Tefnut, as a pendant to representations of Amenhotep IV with the plumes of her consort, the air god Shu (whose name appears in the didactic name of the Aten [but cf. page 53, below]), with his double-crowned images perhaps linking him with the evening-sun god, Atum.

Nefertiti was also represented in sphinx form, as was her husband, in sixty-six pairs that originally formed part of the Karnak Aten complex.[22] These were, however, later decapitated and reworked as ram-headed sphinxes to line the processional way between Pylon X and the Mut complex to the south under Tutankhamun (see page 97, below). Smaller such representations also existed at Karnak.

The Royal Family

As already noted, the king and queen's first child, Princess Meryetaten, appears at Karnak for the first time following the jubilee. This suggests that by this time she was felt likely to survive, and perhaps involved in the ritual once she was able to walk and accompany her parents in official appearances.[23] Although very young, she is shown in such reliefs as a miniature version of her mother, albeit with a sidelock of youth. In a small number of scenes at Karnak, a second princess, Meketaten, is shown, suggesting that she had been born after work on the Aten complex was well advanced, so perhaps around Year 3/4 (cf. page 32, below). A third daughter, Ankhesenpaaten, seems to have made her public appearance when work at Karnak was all but complete, as her name only appears once in the surviving texts, while one miniature (unlabeled) depiction of the royal family shows three daughters.[24]

A unique feature of representations of Meryetaten, and also of later daughters of Nefertiti, is that they are given not only their name and titles, but also the gloss "born of the King's Great Wife (Neferneferuaten-)Nefertiti." Since there is no indication that there was any other royal wife during the first part of the reign, this specification seems of no obvious utility—and has no parallels even when kings did have multiple contemporaneous spouses (e.g., Rameses II). All one can suggest is that it could be seen as a further indication of the exceptional status of Nefertiti, making her maternity as important as the princesses' (implicit) paternity by the king.[25]

The motif of "royal family"—the king, queen, and daughters—became a fundamental icon of the new ideological world that accompanied the rise of the Aten cult. Hitherto, reward by the king had been a regular feature of the decoration of the tomb chapels of the Eighteenth Dynasty, but now this and the wider activities of the royal family would become the principal subject of the decoration of such monuments. This was to the exclusion of the so-called daily life scenes found since the Old Kingdom and most of the other icons that had evolved during the Middle and New Kingdoms, and thus represented a fundamental change. Little material survives from the earliest years of the reign, but in the aforementioned chapel of Ramose (TT55) is perhaps the earliest example of an "Atenist" reward scene to be found. This was placed directly opposite the "classical" reward scene featuring Amenhotep IV and Maat, the contrast between the two scenes underlining the groundbreaking changes that were now being wrought in Egyptian art (fig. 24).

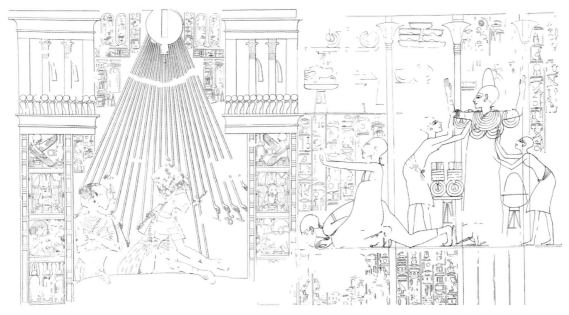

FIGURE 24 "Revolutionary" style depiction of Amenhotep IV and Nefertiti rewarding Ramose in his tomb chapel (TT55).

The Horizon of the Aten

Although significant resources had been put into the building of the Aten complex at Karnak, it had clearly been regarded as but the first phase of a much wider project. Thus, by Year 4 the decision seems to have been taken to found a whole new city to act as both the home of the Aten cult and the new principal royal residence. This could almost have been seen as a "relaunch" of the reign, as it was accompanied by the king changing his nomen to "Akhenaten"—marking him as the "effective spirit" (perhaps even "incarnation") of the Aten.

The chosen location for the new city was in Middle Egypt, across the river from Ashmunein (Hermopolis), cult center of Thoth, and just south of the Old/Middle Kingdom cemeteries of Deir el-Bersha and Sheikh Said (figs. 25, 26, 36). Known anciently as Akhet-Aten ("Horizon of the Aten"), and in modern times as Tell el-Amarna, its limits were set by a series of boundary stelae, the first set recording events dated to IV *prt* 13 in Year 5.[26]

The boundary stelae originally comprised a single pair on the east bank, marking the northern (X) and southern (M, soon replaced by K [fig. 27]) limits of the city. In their texts, it is stated that the king stood at a particular spot at the site chosen for Akhet-Aten (perhaps at the location later occupied by the Small Aten Temple—fig. 28),[27] made offerings to the Aten, and made a proclamation to an assembly of courtiers.[28] This established his city on a site that he had found "not being the property of a god, nor being the property of a goddess, nor being the property of a ruler, nor being the property of a female ruler, nor being the property of any people able to lay claim to it." The stelae included a scene of the king, queen, and Meryetaten worshiping the Aten, to which the figure of Meketaten was added secondarily, reinforcing the idea of her birth around Year 4.

As to *why* the king was taking this step, the relevant section of the proclamation is badly broken and has given rise to a variety of interpretations. The king states that *something* was "worse than those that I heard in Year 4" (and also in Years 1, 2, and 3), and worse than had been heard by three earlier kings: the names are all damaged and only the last can be read with any clarity—giving the prenomen of either Thutmose III or IV. It then notes that the *something* was worse than those "heard by any kings who had assumed the White Crown." The following section seems to talk about "offensive" speech against the Aten (although this is not wholly clear). Accordingly, it would appear that hostility toward the new order had contributed to the decision to move, but its detail remains obscure.

Sanctuaries and sunshades

As well as fixing the unchangeable boundaries of Akhet-Aten, the proclamation decreed the building of its principal sanctuaries: "the 'House of the Aten' . . . , the 'Mansion of the Aten' . . . and the 'House-of-Rejoicing' for the Aten, my father . . . ." These are the

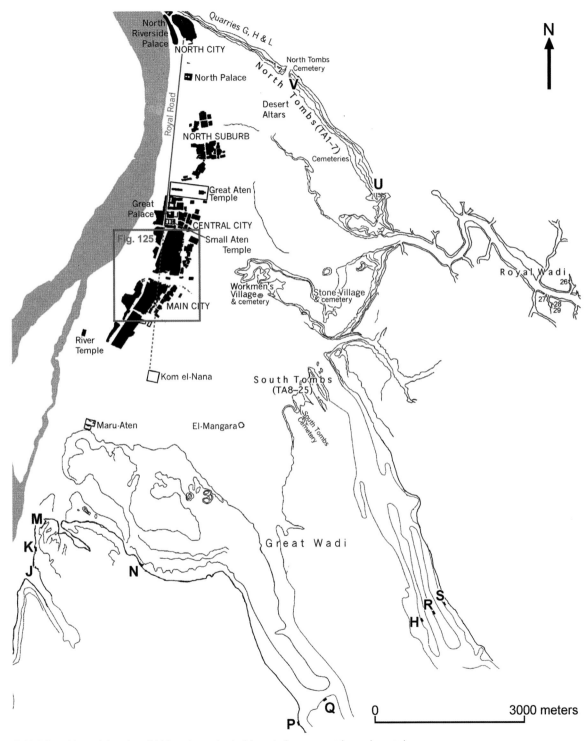

FIGURE 25 Map of the city of Akhet-Aten; the bold capitals represent boundary stelae.

FIGURE 26 View of the desolation that is now the city of Amarna, seen from the North Tombs.

FIGURE 27 Boundary Stela K at Amarna.

FIGURE 28 View from the Small Aten Temple at Amarna to the Royal Wadi.

structures known today as the Small Aten Temple, the Great Aten Temple, and the latter's sanctuary. Also specified was "the Sunshade of the [King's Great] Wife [Neferneferuaten Nefertiti]." In the context of Amarna, such "sunshades" were a special kind of chapel dedicated to female members of the royal family, although the term was also used more generally for sun sanctuaries in royal memorial temples.[29] Later, one would be constructed at Amarna for Kiya, subsequently usurped for Meryetaten (see pages 60, 66, below).[30]

Nefertiti's sunshade lay at what is now known as Kom el-Nana (fig. 30).[31] This lies at the southern end of an axis (see fig. 25) that begins at the very north of the Amarna site, in what would become the Northern City, which included the North Riverside Palace (fig. 86), apparently the royal family's principal residence. The axis then runs in a straight line southward, passing close to a further (North) palace (fig. 29), and then through the heart of the Central City, with the two main Aten Temples fronting onto it and the Great Palace straddling it. This section would become the "Royal Road," but beyond this point housing rapidly grew up, leaving Kom el-Nana isolated, seemingly without any form of ceremonial access from the north.[32]

Kom el-Nana was enclosed by a buttressed mud-brick enclosure wall, with pylon entrances in the west, south, and east, but apparently not north, the whole being 220 meters square. The enclosure was subdivided into a northern section 88 meters deep, and a southern one 122 meters deep, both with gardens, including pits for trees. The southern sector was focused on the so-called South Shrine, some 27 meters wide, built of stone—using large blocks, rather than talatat—and once extensively decorated.[33] On the basis of the style of its reliefs and the presence therein of only the three elder daughters, this southern sector seems to have been constructed early in the building process at Amarna.[34] Its western front had a colonnade of at least two rows of papyrus-bundle

FIGURE 29 The North
Palace at Amarna.

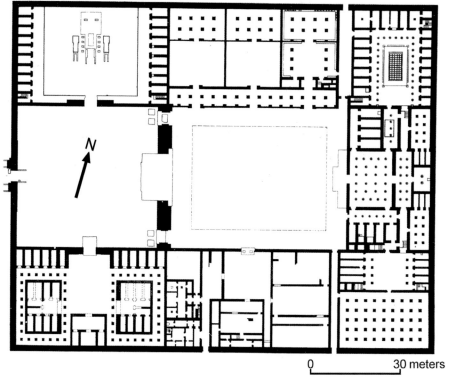

0   30 meters

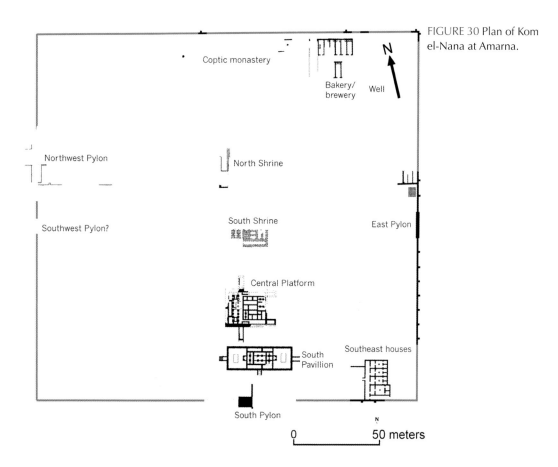

Coptic monastery

Bakery/
brewery   Well

N

Northwest Pylon

North Shrine

Southwest Pylon?

South Shrine

East Pylon

Central Platform

South
Pavillion

Southeast houses

South Pylon

0   50 meters

N

FIGURE 30 Plan of Kom
el-Nana at Amarna.

columns. It was supplemented by the "Central Platform" of mud brick, 1.5 meters high, covering 24.5 by 21.75 meters, and topped by a columned hall and a number of rooms. On the other hand, while the eastern part contained a number of buildings, including houses, the western area of the enclosure seems to have been a mud-floored open court devoid of structures.

Much of the contents of the northern sector were later obliterated by the construction of a Coptic monastery, but remains of a stone "North Shrine" in the southern half and a large brick one in the north have been identified. It is possible that the actual sunshade of Nefertiti lay in this part of the complex, as a subset of the *rwd-'nḫw-itn*, which may have been the name for whole of Kom el-Nana.[35] Nevertheless, it is clear that the sunshade of Nefertiti was an important part of the Kom el-Nana complex.[36] Also decreed were "the residence of Pharaoh" and "the residence of the King's Great Wife." The former was probably the Great Palace, and the latter perhaps the aforementioned North Palace (fig. 29), although nothing survives to confirm its ownership by Nefertiti: indeed, the only known inscription, on the jamb of an inner room, names just Meryetaten.

Houses of eternity and the beyond

Looking beyond this world, Akhenaten continued:

> Let a tomb be made for me in the eastern mountain of Akhet-Aten. Let my burial
> be made in it, in the millions of jubilees that the Aten, my father, has decreed for
> me. Let the burial of the King's Great Wife, Nefertiti, be made in it, in the millions
> of years which the Aten, my father, decreed for her. Let the burial [of] the King's
> Daughter, Meryetaten, [be made] in it, in these millions of years. If I die in any
> town downstream, to the south, to the west, to the east in these millions of years,
> let me be brought (here), so that I may be buried in Akhet-Aten. If the King's
> Great Wife Nefertiti—may she live—dies in any town downstream, to the south,
> to the west, to the east in these millions [of years, let her be brought here, so that]
> she [may be buried in Akhet-Aten. If the King's Daughter Meryetaten dies] in any
> town downstream, to the south, to the west, to the east in the millions of years, let
> her be brought here, so that she may be buried in Akhet-Aten. Let a cemetery for
> the Mnevis Bull [be made] in the eastern mountain of Akhet-Aten, that he may
> [be buried] in it. Let the tomb chapels for the Greatest of Seers, for the God's
> Fathers of the [. . .] Aten be made in the eastern mountain of Akhet-Aten, that
> they may be buried in it. Let [the tombs] of the priests of the [Aten] be [made in
> the eastern mountain of Akhet-Aten] that they may b[e bur]ied in it.

The latter tombs (fig. 31) lay in the cliffs and foothills of the mountain that defined
the eastern boundary of the city, while that which was intended to accommodate the
king, queen, and princess royal was located at the end of a long wadi that ran farther east
into the high desert (fig. 32). This "Royal Wadi" lay on the axis of the Small Aten Temple,
and its mouth closely resembled the $3\underline{h}t$ sign, seemingly defining it as the focus of the
new city. Indeed, the Royal Tomb itself seems to have been regarded as a key focal point,
since the extended axes of both this temple and the Great Aten Temple, 450 meters
farther to the north, bracket the site of the tomb. Within the constraints of ancient sur-
veying, the axes may even have been intended to cross at it.

The Royal Tomb (TA26—fig. 33)[37] differed from almost all earlier and later such
sepulchers in having specific provision for burials other than that of the king himself—a
feature shared with the tomb of Akhenaten's father Amenhotep III (WV22). Traces on
the walls of the main corridor indicate that up to six suites, in addition to the main burial
chamber, were envisaged, although only two were begun. One (α–γ) was ultimately used
for the interment of daughters of Akhenaten and Nefertiti (but not Meryetaten—see
pages 63–65, below). The other may have been intended for Nefertiti, although it was
never finished and was never inscribed (fig. 34).

FIGURE 31 The North (top) and South (bottom) Tombs at Amarna.

FIGURE 32 The Amarna Royal Wadi, from tomb TA27.

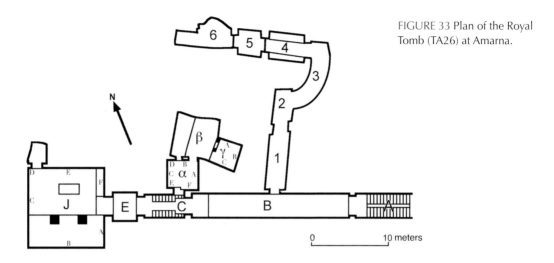

FIGURE 33 Plan of the Royal Tomb (TA26) at Amarna.

FIGURE 34 Chambers 4–5 of the Royal Tomb, probably intended for Nefertiti as queen.

As well as an intended occupant of the tomb, Nefertiti had a further role: goddess of the dead. Akhenaten's sarcophagus (fig. 35) differed from those of his immediate predecessors, which had been made with the plan of a cartouche, in being of rectangular form, with images of the rayed disk of his god on the four sides and the corners enfolded by protective female figures. In the latter, it followed a pattern established for royal canopic chests back in the time of Amenhotep II, the images in question being of the tutelary goddesses Isis, Nephthys, Neith, and Selqet. However, Akhenaten's religious revolution excluded the traditional gods of burial, with the result that Nefertiti became here the protectress of her dead husband—and perhaps the wider dead as well. On the other hand, the scarcity of material from the period directly bearing on mortuary belief makes generalizations problematic. As the sarcophagus of Akhenaten was begun before Year 9, on the basis of the forms of Aten cartouches used on it (cf. pages 50, 53–54, below), it is clear that Nefertiti's funerary role came early in the reign.

FIGURE 35 The sarcophagus of Akhenaten, restored from fragments (Cairo TR3/3/70/2).

Building the city

A year after the "First Proclamation," Akhenaten delivered a further declaration (the "Later Proclamation") from "the southeastern mountain of Akhet-Aten," having departed from the "pavilion of matting" that currently represented the royal accommodation in the just-begun city. It essentially reconfirmed the provisions of what is now generally termed the "Earlier Proclamation" of the previous year, including a repetition of the statement that the city limits of Akhet-Aten were immutable[38] and a more detailed exposition of those limits. These were delineated by a new series of twelve (known) additional boundary stelae A, B, F, H, J, N, P, Q, R, S, U and V (fig. 36).[39]

Rather than just marking the north and south riverside boundaries of Akhet-Aten as the earlier stelae had done, the new markers were also placed farther inland. The latter were cut into the northern (V and U) and southern (N) arcs of cliffs and also in the wadis to the far southeast (H, P, Q, R, and S), apparently the area in which this Later Proclamation was made. In addition, stelae A, B, and F were placed in the cliffs and foothills on the west bank to confirm the annexation of a vast swath of agricultural land on the other side of the Nile to feed the new settlement on the then largely barren east bank. These "Later" stelae were more elaborate than the "Early" ones, with a more extensively decorated lunette and a series of subsidiary rock-cut statues of the king, queen,

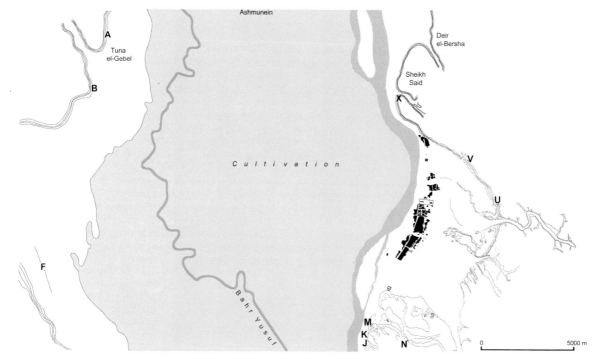

FIGURE 36 Map of Greater Amarna, showing the west bank agricultural land that supported the city on the largely barren east.

and their two eldest daughters (fig. 37). An image of Ankhesenpaaten was added to the subsidiary sculptures of stelae A, B, P, Q, and U, suggesting that she was born while these stelae were being carved in Year 6/7.

As already noted, the royal family were central to the new religious outlook, standing as the principal intermediaries between humankind and the deity, dominating the surviving blocks from the temples of Amarna (figs. 38, 39, 40). But it was not only in temples that the key role of the king, queen, and their children in the Aten cult was manifest. Many of the major private houses in the city had chapels[40] in which the object of devotion was not the physical sun above but a stela or shrine showing the royal family adoring the sun on the behalf of the worshiper (fig. 41), or simply of the royal family in a domestic context (fig. 42). They also displaced almost all of the traditional scenes in the tomb chapels of private individuals, whose walls were now dominated by scenes of the activities of the royal family—worshiping the Aten, traveling from the North Riverside Palace to the Central City, rewarding the tomb owner (figs. 43, 44). In all these cases, Nefertiti is shown alongside the king and her daughters, the number of whom continued to grow over the time the tomb chapels were decorated, which seems to have been primarily during the half decade directly following the foundation of the city.

a

b   c   d

FIGURE 37 a. Boundary Stela U. b. & c. Depictions of Nefertiti from Boundary Stelae P (MFA 34.49) and N (Kansas City 44-56). d. Head of Nefertiti from Boundary Stela Q (Melbourne, National Gallery of Victoria 616-D2).

FIGURE 38 Balustrade showing Akhenaten and Nefertiti in the earlier "revolutionary" style; from Amarna, Great Palace (Cairo TR30/10/26/12).

FIGURE 39 Nefertiti, as depicted on a fragment of column; from Amarna Great Palace (Ashmolean AN1893.1-45[73]).

FIGURE 40 Akhenaten, Nefertiti, and Meryetaten, as depicted on a fragment of column; from Amarna Great Palace (Ashmolean AN1893.1-45[75]).

FIGURE 41 Façade of a shrine from the official residence of Panehsy, Amarna T.41.1 (Cairo JE65041 + San Diego).

FIGURE 42 Relief, probably from a household shrine, showing Akhenaten, Nefertiti, and their three eldest daughters; probably from Amarna (Berlin ÄM14145).

FIGURE 43 North wall of the hall of the tomb chapel of Meryre i (TA4) at Amarna, showing the journey of the royal family from the North City to the Central City.

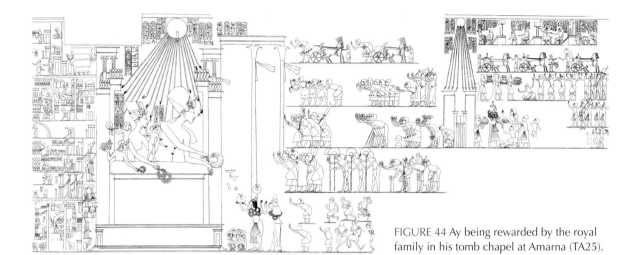

FIGURE 44 Ay being rewarded by the royal family in his tomb chapel at Amarna (TA25).

FIGURE 45 The six daughters of Akhenaten and Nefertiti, as shown in the tomb chapel of Meryre ii (TA2; see also fig. 67), with restoration after early copies.

Nefertiti's Children

While the three eldest girls are depicted in all the Amarna tomb chapels that preserve the appropriate scenes, the fourth daughter, Neferneferuaten-tasherit, appears for the first time in the tomb of Panehsy (TA6).[41] After this, she is then to be seen in those of Meryre i (TA4), Huya (TA1), and Meryre ii (TA2),[42] suggesting that she was born a little after the move to Amarna. Two further girls, Neferneferure and Setepenre, only appear in one tomb chapel: that of Meryre ii, perhaps the latest of all the decorated private tombs at Amarna. Interestingly, while Neferneferure is seen twice in this tomb, Setepenre is found just once, in a scene explicitly dated to Year 12 (fig. 45; for the whole scene, see fig. 67), suggesting her birth took place only a little before. The five eldest girls all appear in a now fragmentary painting from the King's House in company with their parents (fig. 46, but there seems no sign of Setepenre,[43] suggesting that the scene was painted before her birth).

The replacement of "-Aten" in the names of the final two daughters by "-Re," invoking a more traditional aspect of the sun, may indicate that they were born after the reform suggested by a change in the didactic name of the Aten around Year 9 (see pages 50, 53–54, below). The youngest three girls are thus likely to have been born during Years 7/8 through

FIGURE 46 Fragment of wall painting, which originally showed the king, queen, and (probably) five of their daughters, two of whom survive; from Amarna, King's House (Ashmolean AN1893.1-41[267]).

10/11. As well as in tombs, the family also appears on the aforementioned house stelae and likewise in paintings from the royal palaces, and is often shown in an informal manner unheard of at any other time in Egyptian history (figs. 42, 46, 47). The daughters were also depicted in three dimensions, various heads and other fragments of which have survived (figs. 48, 49).

The question of whether the couple had any male children has been much debated. The key piece of monumental evidence for Akhenaten having a son is a block that formerly formed part of a temple wall at Amarna,[44] although it was found at Ashmunein along with a huge number of blocks from the site. These blocks had been reused in the foundations of a pylon of the temple of Thoth during the time of Rameses II.[45] It names a "King's Son of his Body, his beloved, Tutankhuaten" (fig. 50, left); while the *w* is not found in writings of the king Tutankhaten/amun, it seems certain that this prince was indeed the later pharaoh.

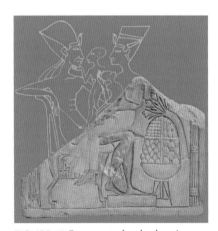

FIGURE 47 Fragment of stela showing Nefertiti on the lap of Akhenaten; probably from a household shrine at Amarna (Louvre E11624).

FIGURE 48 Quartzite head from a composite statue of one of the Amarna princesses; from Amarna house P47.1 or 2 (Berlin ÄM21223).

FIGURE 49 Fragment of a quartzite statuette of an Amarna female; from Amarna (Louvre E25409).

The adjoining block, with its text facing in the opposite direction, names the "King's Daughter of his Body, his [beloved], Praised by the Lord of the Two Lands, [. . .]A[ten]";[46] given that the Ashmunein blocks seem to date to the latter part of the reign, it is probable that the latter name should be restored "[Ankhesenpa]a[ten]."[47] The blocks clearly provided labels for adjacent images of the prince and princess who, on the basis of the orientation of the hieroglyphs, would have been facing each other. No blocks have yet been identified as attributable to the rest of the tableau, but one assumes that it would have comprised the king and queen, accompanied by the two children, worshiping the Aten, with the queen (perhaps now a "crowned-queen" or even a female king: see pages 71–79, below) and one of the children on the left, and the king and the other child on the right (fig. 51). As such it would have been the earliest known example of a prince being shown on a temple wall purely by virtue of being a king's son, rather than as the holder of a substantive office.

This situation can be traced back to the Old Kingdom,[48] and certainly applied down to the time of Amenhotep III—as is shown by the fact that in the First Jubilee reliefs at Soleb the king is shown with Queen Tiye and Princesses Sitamun, Iset, and Henuttaneb, but with no sign of Prince Amenhotep, by then heir to the throne.[49] This suggests that some conceptual change in millennia-old royal representative decorum took place during the latter part of Akhenaten's reign.

While the block does not explicitly call Tutankh(u)aten the son of Akhenaten, the latter is the only king known to be named on blocks from Amarna temples, and was certainly the father of the princess. Accordingly, that he was implicitly the father of the prince named in the same scene seems all but certain.[50] One would also at first assume that the mothers of the two younger people might be the same—thus suggesting that Nefertiti was Tutankhamun's mother (unfortunately, the element of the texts that would have given their maternity is missing).

FIGURE 50 Blocks from Amarna, reused at Ashmunein, naming Ankhesenpaaten and Tutankhuaten.

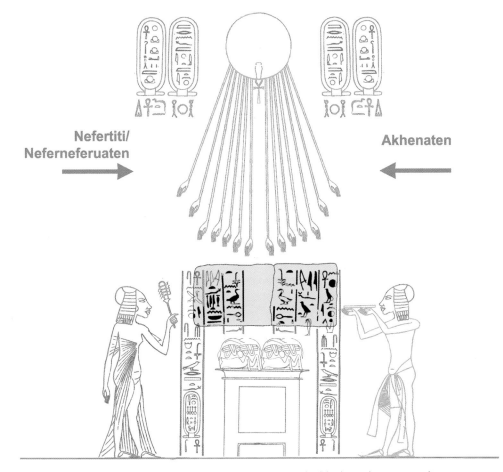

Nefertiti/
Neferneferuaten

Akhenaten

FIGURE 51 Tentative reconstruction of the scene incorporating the blocks in the previous figure.

This has, however, been widely doubted on the basis of the lack of any unequivocal representation of Tutankh(u)aten with Nefertiti, for example along with her daughters in tomb or temple scenes. However, this can be easily explained by the long-standing previous decorum of not showing royal sons in official contexts purely by virtue of birth, and ignores the fact that the Ashmunein blocks come from the *first ever* depiction of its kind—and that, if correctly restored, they may indeed have shown Nefertiti and Tutankh(u)aten together. Accordingly, and supported by the interpretation of the genetic data discussed in chapter 1, it seems most likely that Tutankh(u)aten was the son of Akhenaten and Nefertiti.

As for the date of Tutankh(u)aten's birth, this depends on the view one takes of events following Akhenaten's death—whether Tutankh(u)aten succeeded him directly or after an intervening reign. If the latter, given that Tutankhamun died at the age of eighteen after a reign of nine years, his birth would have taken place around Akhenaten's Year 11 (which could also explain his omission from extant tomb chapel royal family scenes, which seem to only go up to Year 12). If he did succeed directly (as is argued in chapter 3), his birth would be brought forward to around Year 8, either between his future wife Ankhesenpaaten and Neferneferuaten-tasherit or between the latter and Neferneferure—assuming, of course, no multiple births.

The Other Wife

We have already briefly met Kiya, the other known wife of Akhenaten, noting that she held a title, Greatly Beloved Wife of the King, that appears never to have been borne by any other individual in Egyptian history. Her origins are wholly unknown, although, like Nefertiti, there have been speculations that she might have been a foreigner—perhaps even the Mitannian Tadukhepa (notwithstanding the issues already raised over the latter being Nefertiti; see pages 17–18, 113–14).[51] An exotic origin might help explain her nonstandard title.

The date of Kiya's marriage to Akhenaten is unknown, but must have been before the change in the names of the Aten around Year 9, owing to the earlier Aten-name's presence on a number of objects belonging to her. She was depicted on temple walls at Amarna and also had a sunshade in the complex known as Maru-Aten.[52] On the former she was depicted with a single female child (figs. 52, 53, bottom), whose name seems nowhere to be preserved,[53] although there have been suggestions that she might have been the Princess Beketaten who is usually seen as the youngest daughter of Amenhotep III and Tiye.[54]

Study of Kiya is hampered by the fact that she fell into disgrace—the cause or nature of this being wholly obscure—some time during the latter years of the reign. This was certainly after Year 11, when she is named on a wine-jar docket,[55] and probably after Year 12, on the basis of a block from Ashmunein naming her that includes an epithet

FIGURE 52 Block reused at Ashmunein, probably showing Akhenaten, Kiya, and their daughter.

FIGURE 53 Top: Akhenaten and Kiya sacrificing ducks; Kiya's head shape has been remodeled and her label text amended to name Meryetaten (MMA 1985.28.2 + Ny Carlsberg ÆIN 1776); bottom: Akhenaten offers to the Aten, in the presence of a single daughter; the relief is datable stylistically to the latter part of the king's reign. The comprehensive erasure of the girl's titles and name, but with her features left undamaged, suggests that she may have been Kiya's daughter, with the never fulfilled intention of substituting a text naming Meryetaten or Ankhesenpaaten carved into plaster (Brooklyn 60.197.6); blocks reused at Ashmunein.

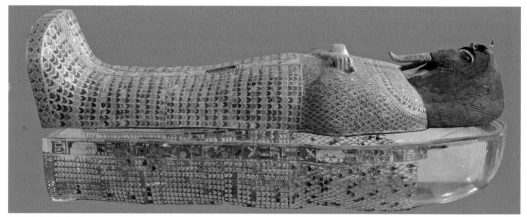

FIGURE 54 Coffin from KV55, made for Kiya, and later adapted for the burial of a king, almost certainly Smenkhkare (Cairo JE39627).

apparently only adopted by Akhenaten after Year 12.[56] Her coffin and canopic jars—made before Year 9—were subsequently reused for the burial of a king who seems to have been Smenkhkare (figs. 54, 55; see pages 69–70, below). Kiya's disgrace thus must have preceded the latter's death—which may have occurred around Year 14 (cf. page 70). Kiya's other monuments were also usurped, mainly for Meryetaten (figs. 55, 125) and occasionally for Ankhesenpaaten (see further pages 66–67). The fact that Meryetaten was still a princess when these changes were made indicates that Kiya's disgrace occurred before Meryetaten transitioned to being a queen, which appears to have happened around Year 13 (see pages 68–69, below). The fact that nothing was taken over in the name of Meketaten would indicate that Kiya's disgrace fell after her death (for which, see below, pages 63–66).

Aten and the Gods

Following the formal establishment of Akhet-Aten in Years 4/5, no specific dates can be attributed to events during the first half-dozen years of the city's existence, which presumably saw its progressive construction, occupation, and expansion. However, somewhere during this time the cartouche names of the Aten underwent a fundamental change. Rather than being, as had been the case since the death of Amenhotep III, "Living-Re-Horakhty-who-rejoices-in-the-Horizon-in-his-name-Shu-Re-who-is-in-Aten," the god becomes "Living-Re-Ruler-of-the-Two-Horizons-Rejoicing-in-the-Horizon-in-his-Name-of-Re-the-Father-who-Returns-as-Aten."[57] The key change here is that the old air god Shu is dropped from the Aten's nature, as is the explicit link with Re-Horakhty, seen in the Aten's original anthropomorphic manifestation.

The change seems to have happened between Year 8, when the original form was still being used in a "colophon" that was then added to Boundary Stelae A and B,[58] and

Year 12, when the "Later" form appears in dated tableaux in two Amarna tombs.[59] It has generally been assumed that the change actually took place in Year 9, on the basis that the new name first appears in the tomb chapel of Panehsy (TA6), which seems to have been in the process of decoration at the time of the birth of Neferneferuaten-tasherit—probably born in Year 8/9 (page 46, above), but this is by no means certain. Nevertheless, it seems clear that much of the construction of the city of Akhet-Aten and its necropoleis was well under way by the time that the change took place, clearly marking an evolution in Akhenaten's theological thinking.[60]

We have already noted the way in which Nefertiti had superseded the traditional female deities of burial and that, while amulets of traditional household deities have been found in the workmen's villages and cemeteries at Amarna,[61] there are no signs of any divinity other than the sun among the "royal" monuments there. The only exception would be the citation of Shu in the early Aten names—although this could have actually been meant as the physical "air" or "atmosphere," rather than the god himself.[62] If indeed the god, the change in the Aten's name could be seen as a shift toward a more austerely monotheist conception of the Aten.

As such, the change has been suggested as the launch point of a key episode of Akhenaten's reign—the proscription of the god Amun. Under this, images of the god were the subject of widespread erasure (fig. 56). The god's name suffered similarly, even when incorporated into the name of a person, the whole of such a theophoric name sometimes being destroyed as "collateral damage." Even Amenhotep III had his entire nomen erased in a number of cases. However, while many have taken the view that it took place early in Akhenaten's reign—either with the change of Aten names, or even earlier—others have argued that it took place not long before Akhenaten's death. In favor of a mid or late date is that the vulture of Amun's consort, Mut, an icon generally also erased as part of the proscription process, was included as part of the name of Nefertiti's sister Mutnedjmet in a number of

FIGURE 55 Canopic jar from KV55, likewise originally manufactured for Kiya, whose name and titles were erased some time before the piece was finally taken over for its final owner (MMA 30.8.54).

FIGURE 56 Block originally from the memorial temple of Amenhotep III, showing the erasure of a figure of Amun; later reused in the south pylon of the memorial temple of Merenptah.

Amarna tomb-chapels decorated soon after the move to Amarna.[63] Supporting a date after Year 9 is the fact that a funerary shrine made for Queen Tiye was made bearing not only the Later form of the god's name, but also Amenhotep III's Amun-citing nomen—although the "Amun" element was subsequently removed.[64] Indeed, it may be that for some considerable time, while Aten was regarded as the king's pre-eminent god, there was effectively (albeit probably implicitly) a cohabitation with Amun, until some event prompted the radical change in the king's approach to the King of the Gods.

Curiously, no gods outside the Theban triad seem to have been significantly affected by direct action,[65] although the retrospective Restoration Stela of Tutankhamun (see pages 86–87, below) suggests that non-Aten sanctuaries may have been starved of resources. At first sight this passivity seems to sit strangely with the active erasure of the plural "gods" in some contexts. However, this seems essentially to have been in the context of Amun's title of "King of the Gods," and one wonders whether here we have the clue to Akhenaten's antipathy toward Amun—the latter's claim to dominion over other deities. If one thing is clear from the Great Hymn to the Aten, found in a number of tomb chapels at Amarna and seemingly setting out the key tenets of the Atenist creed,[66] it is the sun god's status as the creator and sustainer of life and implicit standing as supreme god. Against this background it may be that it was Amun's pretentions to be supreme deity that led to his being targeted for explicit persecution.

We may thus perceive something other than the absolute monotheism of a jealous god that has often been imputed to Akhenaten. What that *something* actually was has been much discussed, but it does seem that Akhenaten's monolatry of the Aten may provide the least unsound basis for analysis: that he *worshiped* a single god, without any necessary implication of his *believing* that there was but one god.[67]

Representing the Queen

As we have already noted (pages 11–12,), the first known representations of Nefertiti were in a "classical" style, even when paired with her husband in "revolutionary" style. However, this soon changed, albeit in stages, to the latter, which was then extended to his family, and then to everyone else (figs. 9–11). The meaning of the "revolutionary" Amarna style has been much debated,[68] but given the context of its appearance alongside the growth of the Aten cult, and the appearance of the nonanthropomorphic form of the god, the idea that it was part of establishing a "Year Zero" across a whole swath of material culture seems persuasive. That in its early phases it seemed to subvert everything about the way that the human form was represented, including seemingly making the royal couple facially as "ugly" as possible, is consistent with a truly "revolutionary" approach, part of whose purpose was to underline that everything had now changed. This kind of "shock value" can be seen in a range of such contexts—for example, in the images presented by the punk rock movement in the late 1970s. That the new style began with just the king is suggestive of the idea that it began with an exaggeration, indeed caricature, of certain aspects of his own physique, as a means of setting him apart from the rest of humanity as principal intermediary with his god—although by no means as the "pathological" specimen that has often been alleged.[69]

Yet such parallels often follow such an "in your face" initial phase with a "consolidation" one. In these, the rough edges of the initial "revolutionary" approach are smoothed out and a new style is produced that remains true to the underlying concepts but restores some of the "prerevolutionary" aesthetic in the consolidated style (as "new wave" followed punk musically). This was certainly the case in the Amarna style, where the distortions of the early phases are followed by a naturalism, and indeed elegance, that would both continue into the "postrevolutionary" styles of the reigns of Akhenaten's immediate successors and influence even early Rameside art.

This can be well traced when looking at two-dimensional representations of Nefertiti, particularly comparing figs. 38–42, all dating to the first part of Akhenaten's reign, with fig. 57, which will have been produced toward its end. In three-dimensional art, we are hampered by the paucity of surviving material from the earlier part of the reign, with only the Karnak colossi (fig. 23) to work with—although the facial distortions of these

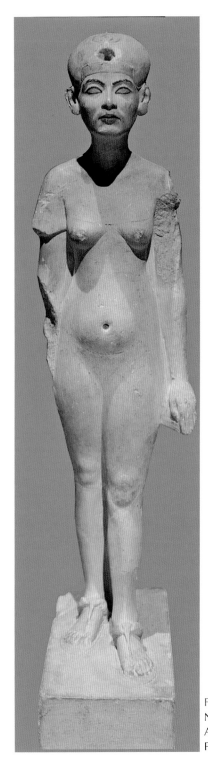

FIGURE 57 "Trial piece" with the profiles of (probably) Akhenaten and Nefertiti, in the more refined style of the latter part of the king's reign; purchased at Amarna in 1881 (Brooklyn 16.48).

FIGURE 58 Limestone statuette of Nefertiti during the latter part of Akhenaten's reign; from Amarna P.47.2 (Berlin ÄM21263).

FIGURE 59 Akhenaten and Nefertiti (Louvre E15593).

FIGURE 60 Fragment of indurated limestone statue of Nefertiti; from Great Temple at Amarna (MMA 21.9.4).

pieces are quite clear, they are probably exacerbated by the intent that the faces be viewed looking up from below, resulting in an unnatural alignment of the ears.[70] However, from the latter part of the reign we have a considerable amount of material that gives an idea of the trajectory of developments in such works.

Although a number of smaller pieces, perhaps intended for private chapels, have survived intact or in relatively good condition (e.g., figs. 58, 59), no monumental statues survive intact from Amarna. Many were smashed in antiquity (fig. 60), sometimes to smithereens;[71] at best they were decapitated (figs. 49, 61).

A large corpus of heads, many usually characterized as sculptor's models for use when creating statues for public display, comes (along with other items of sculpture) from Amarna houses P47.2 (attributed to the sculptor Thutmose—fig. 121), O47.16A, and O47.20.[72] Dating from the latter years of Akhenaten's reign (indeed, the workshop seems to have still been in use in Year 1 of Tutankhamun),[73] the heads mark a further moving-on from the revolutionary Amarna style to a "mature" variant, which replaces the distortions of the former with a more naturalistic approach while still retaining

FIGURE 61 Limestone statue of Nefertiti making offerings (BM EA935).

FIGURE 62 Painted limestone bust of Nefertiti; from Amarna house P47.2 (Berlin ÄM21300).

the underlying features of the style. They include some of the most famous representations of the period, including *the* most famous of all: the painted bust of Nefertiti (fig. 62).[74]

A feature of the art of the Amarna Period is the extensive creation of "composite" statues, which were made up of a variety of stones that could self-color the resulting pieces.[75] Thus, clothing would be made from white limestone or calcite, with flesh made from quartzite, whose tone beautifully matched the golden-brown skin tone of many Egyptians; eyes would be made from calcite, obsidian, faience, and glass. Owing to the hardness of the material, a significant number of heads survive, perhaps the finest being an unfinished example of Nefertiti herself (fig. 63).[76] However, this is rivaled by a complete example (probably Nefertiti, but perhaps Meryetaten) from Memphis, albeit devoid of its inlays (fig. 64). This technique was also used for two-dimensional art, with elements of reliefs inset into the matrix of the wall or stela (figs. 65, 66).

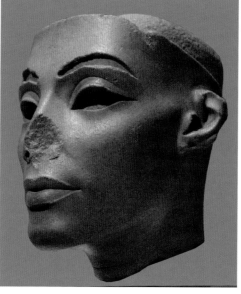

FIGURE 64 Quartzite head of Nefertiti, from a composite statue; from Memphis/Kom el-Qala (Cairo JE45547).

FIGURE 63 Unfinished quartzite head of Nefertiti, intended for a composite statue; from Amarna O.47.20 (Cairo JE59286).

FIGURE 65 Part of the façade of an element of a sunshade temple dedicated to Meryetaten, with composite reliefs in which key parts were provided in other materials. It was located in a *pr-Wʿ-n-Rʿ*, which may have lain at or near Heliopolis, as it was subsequently reused there as a sphinx base under Merenptah. It was then further reused in the Muski area of Cairo (UPMAA E16230).

Year 12

Year 12, II *prt*, day 8: [the king and queen] appeared on the great carrying-chair of gold to receive the tribute of Kharu [Syria–Palestine] and Kush [Nubia], the West and the East. All countries collected together at one time, and the lands in the midst of the sea, bringing offerings to the king upon the great throne of Akhet-Aten for receiving the goods of every land, granting to them the breath of life.

This text appears as a caption to a tableau occupying the whole of the west wall of the first hall of the tomb chapel of Huya, steward of Queen Tiye (TA1: fig. 67, top). A very similar, but more summary, text is to be found in another large tableau on the east wall of the first room of the next-door tomb chapel of the Royal Scribe Meryre ii (TA2: fig. 67, bottom).

The two tableaux, often called the "durbar" reliefs, complement one another, showing respectively the royal couple's approach to the location of the festivities in their carrying-chair, and their receipt from a kiosk of gifts from the durbar attendees. Both feature extensive depictions of raw materials and manufactured goods, and of manacled individuals—Syrian and Nubian in appearance—brought by several distinct delegations, recognizable iconographically as including Nubians, Syrians, Hittites, and possibly Amorites.

This great international gathering was clearly a particularly significant event in Akhenaten's career, with much of the known world bringing gifts to the king. However, the import of the event itself remains obscure. The precise date given in both label texts shows it to be a record of a specific event, and not a generic icon—but why was it occurring then? It may be that such events took place periodically during the Eighteenth Dynasty, and that it is only because of the exceptional nature of

FIGURE 66 Quartzite face of Nefertiti, from a composite relief; from Great Temple at Amarna (Brooklyn 33.685).

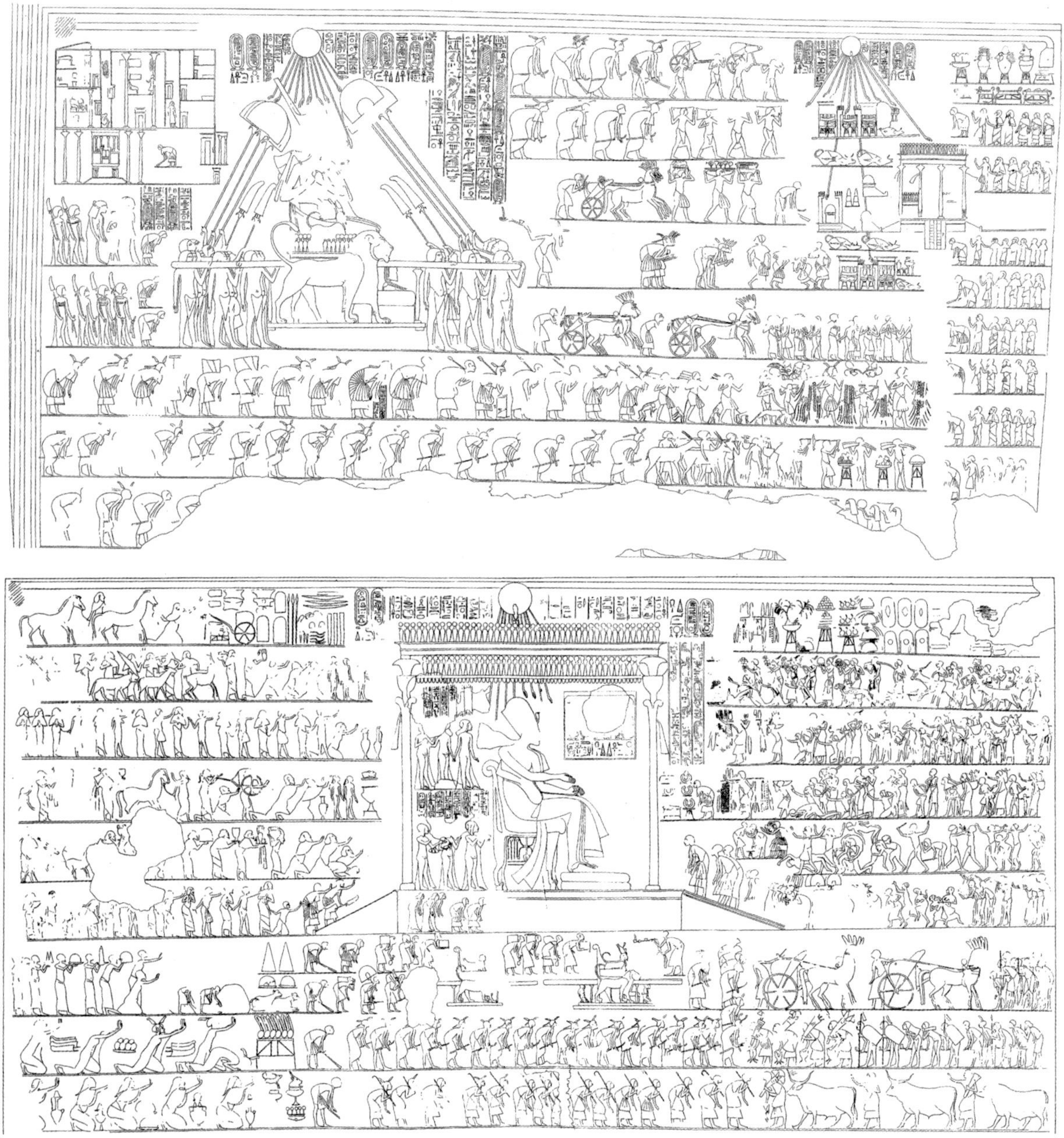

FIGURE 67 The two phases of the Year 12 "durbar" at Amarna, as shown respectively in the tomb chapels of Meryre ii (TA2) and Huya (TA1) at Amarna. In the first, the king and queen proceed on a carrying-chair to the location of the festivities, while in the second, and now accompanied by their daughters (see detail in fig. 45), they receive gifts from many foreign delegations.

Amarna tomb iconography that this particular one is depicted and dated. The breadth of the attendance and the overall context would suggest it was not simply the outcome of a successful military action, although at some time during Years 10–12 Akhenaten's armies had scored a victory somewhere in the vicinity of the Wadi el-Allaqi, about three hundred kilometers east of Wadi Halfa.[77]

One option is to see in it an international celebration of the completion of Akhenaten's great project of the city of Akhet-Aten. Given that work had by now been going on for seven years, might not the king be showing off to the world his model capital city and the glory of the Aten? Nothing about the label texts suggests this—but neither do they imply any of the interpretations that have been put on the event—while the fact that it occurred half a dozen years after the inception of the city would be consistent with likely progress in the construction program. It is now becoming increasingly clear that this process may have cost countless lives. Cemeteries that included at least some workers show early death and signs of having endured heavy physical labor.[78]

The durbar tableau in TA2 shows, as previously noted, all six daughters for the first and only time. It has also been suggested that it also shows Nefertiti, for the first time, further advanced in status by wearing the kingly blue crown (see page 71, below). The traces are, however, marginal, and in at least some representations certainly postdating Year 12 Nefertiti is shown wearing her characteristic flat-topped crown. Nevertheless, within a few years she would indeed advance to "crowned queen"—and not long after to fully fledged female king.

FIGURE 68 Even as "mere" queen, Nefertiti's ongoing exceptional status is shown by her depiction smiting an enemy on the cabin of her barge within a temple scene; from a block from Amarna, reused at Ashmunein (MFA 63.260).

3 To Crowned Queen and Pharaoh

The triumph of Year 12, when the whole world had come to pay homage to the royal couple, must have been seen by them as marking a watershed, beyond which anything might be possible. Yet within a short while the first of a series of tragedies would visit the royal family, and a bare five years after the durbar, Akhenaten himself would be dead.

The first to die seem to have been the youngest girls—Neferneferure and Setepenre. They are almost certainly the two now-nameless individuals shown being mourned by Akhenaten and Nefertiti in scenes added secondarily to the wall of chamber α in the Royal Tomb (figs. 69, 70). They were followed to the grave by Meketaten, for whom a burial chamber (γ) was provided beyond the room now occupied by her younger siblings. It was adorned with scenes of her being mourned, like her sisters, as a corpse on a bier by her parents and, as a standing figure in a bower (figs. 71, 72), by them, Meryetaten, Ankhesenpaaten, and Neferneferuaten-tasherit; the room was equipped with a small granite sarcophagus, its size reflecting the princess's youth.[1]

Much confusion has been caused by the presence in the bier-mourning scenes of a child in the arms of a nurse. On this basis, it has often been asserted that the deceased had died in childbirth. However, the youngest girls were without doubt far too young to have been fertile, while the case for Meketaten is marginal at best. In addition, the circumstances of a person's death are never alluded to in an Egyptian tomb, and it has thus been suggested that the babies may be an Amarna take on the age-old concept of incipient rebirth that underpinned Egyptian funerary beliefs.[2] This is supported by the most credible restoration of the damaged label text that accompanied the baby in Meketaten's

FIGURE 69 Chamber α in the Royal Tomb at Amarna (TA26); the left wall (A) bears a scene of the worship of the rising sun, while that on the right has death scenes of two princesses (F).

FIGURE 70 The upper part of wall F of chamber α, showing a princess being mourned by her parents on the left, with a baby being carried outside the death chamber.

FIGURE 71 Wall of chamber γ, showing the mourning of Meketaten, lying on a bier.

FIGURE 72 Scene on the adjacent wall, showing an effigy of Meketaten, mourned by her parents and Meryetaten, Ankhesenpaaten, and Neferneferuaten-tasherit.

scene, which seems almost certainly to have named the princess herself, rather than any offspring of hers.

As for the actual cause of the princesses' deaths, we have no data, but it has been suggested that the durbar of Year 12 brought not only gifts but also disease to Egypt.[3] Certainly, a decade and a half later, Egyptian prisoners of war taken by the Hittites were suffering from a plague so virulent that it infected and killed many in Anatolia, including the Hittite king himself. The deaths of the three princesses seem to have taken place

FIGURE 73 Two blocks from Amarna and reused at Ashmunein including the names of Meryetaten-tasherit (top) and of Ankhesenpaaten-tasherit (bottom: MMA 1991.237.27).

around the same time as that of the queen mother Tiye, who was also interred in the Royal Tomb,[4] a cluster of deaths within the same family that would certainly be consistent with virulent disease.

Probably to be dated to soon after the death of Meketaten is the disgrace of Kiya, and the replacement of her name and titles with those of others. At Maru-Aten, all changes seem to have been in favor of Meryetaten, indicating that this had been redesignated as her sunshade. On other monuments, represented by the blocks from Ashmunein, a few were altered in favor of Ankhesenpaaten, as well as others for Meryetaten. These substitutions present problems since, besides the names and titles of Kiya being replaced by those of the princesses, the label texts of Kiya's daughter are also replaced by ones citing daughters of both Meryetaten and Ankhesenpaaten, named Meryetaten-tasherit[5] and Ankhesenpaaten-tasherit (fig. 73).[6]

Since there is no evidence for either Meryetaten or Ankhesenpaaten having yet married, significant controversy has arisen: were Meryetaten-tasherit and Ankhesenpaaten-tasherit real? If they were real, were they indeed offspring of Meryetaten and Ankhesenpaaten, and who then were their father(s)? Or were they "phantoms" conjured up to facilitate the easier reworking of the texts of Kiya and her daughter?[7] If real, most have assumed that the father was in both cases Akhenaten, reflecting, for some who reject him as Tutankh(u)aten's father, a "desperation" to sire a son. Yet if so, why were Meryetaten and Ankhesenpaaten not given appropriate "King's Wife" titles to make them suitable mothers for a pharaoh's offspring? Both Amenhotep III and, later, Rameses II, elevated daughters to the status King's Great Wife, although the question of an associated sexual relationship remains moot.

While Meryetaten-tasherit and Ankhesenpaaten-tasherit are explicitly stated, in texts carved from scratch over the original erased ones, to be the bodily offspring of Meryetaten and Ankhesenpaaten, there are chronological problems with accepting such texts at face value. A key issue is that the textual replacements all seem to have taken place at the same time—presumably straight after Kiya's disgrace, given the unlikelihood that raw scars would have been left on temple walls for long. Yet this synchronicity presents major problems if the -tasherits were real, as Ankhesenpaaten was apparently born no earlier than Year 6 (pages 30, 42, above) and thus highly unlikely to have been physically capable of bearing a child before Year 16 at the very earliest.[8] However, by that time Meryetaten was already a queen (see below, pages 68–69). Unless Meryetaten's queenly status had been for some reason ignored in the context of the recuttings (perhaps for symmetry with her sister?), there seems no possibility that the reworking of the Kiya and daughter reliefs can have taken place at a time when both Meryetaten and Ankhesenpaaten were of an appropriate age and status to be real mothers. Another possibility could be, perhaps, to argue that, since Meryetaten could have been fertile prior to her transition to queenship, Meryetaten-tasherit was "real" (and perhaps her child with Smenkhkare, certainly Meryetaten's husband when she became a queen), but that Ankhesenpaaten-tasherit was "invented" to allow Ankhesenpaaten to be included in the recutting scheme. But why there would have been such a need to include Ankhesenpaaten at all would be difficult to explain.

Accordingly, one must seemingly adopt as a least-bad explanation the hypothesis that the recutting of the Ashmunein blocks was done to preserve the integrity of the scenes following the disgrace of Kiya. To avoid making extensive changes to the figures in the reliefs, the names of the king's two senior surviving daughters would have been inserted, together with fictional children of their own. One wonders if this was done with some implication of prospective wishes for fecundity on the part of the princesses who, it may have been assumed, might reproduce at some point during the existence of the building from which the blocks derived.

Smenkhkare and Meryetaten

Meryetaten's aforementioned elevation to queenship occurred when she became the spouse of one of the most wraith-like figures of the whole period: King Ankhkheperure Smenkhkare (cf. pages 128–29, below, for the long-running debates on his identity and even gender). The marriage is attested by two principal sources: an unfinished relief of the two of them in the tomb chapel of Meryre ii (TA2—fig. 74) and a now lost block from Memphis that bore the remains of their names (fig. 75).[9] There are also gold sequins bearing both Smenkhkare's prenomen and the name of Meryetaten, in twin cartouches,[10] found adorning a small linen garment from the tomb of Tutankhamun.[11]

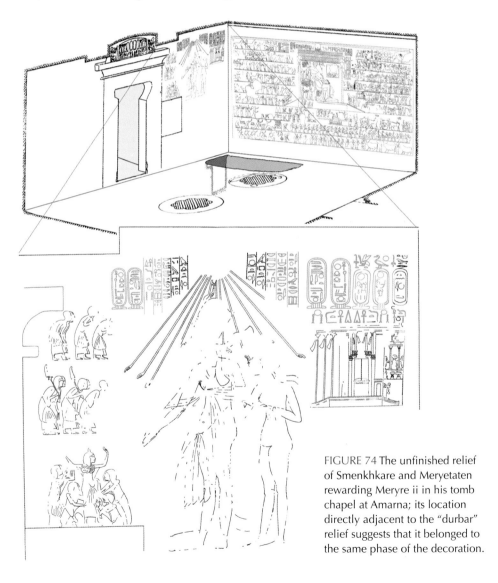

FIGURE 74 The unfinished relief of Smenkhkare and Meryetaten rewarding Meryre ii in his tomb chapel at Amarna; its location directly adjacent to the "durbar" relief suggests that it belonged to the same phase of the decoration.

Smenkhkare's stature as a coruler alongside Akhenaten is suggested by the existence of a jar bearing their two names.[12] Moreover, that the association was in place by around Year 13/14 is suggested by the location of the TA2 relief directly adjacent to the Year 12 "durbar" tableau[13] and perhaps also by the presence of a ring bezel with the prenomen of Smenkhkare in the same context at the Small Aten Temple as a potsherd bearing the date of Year 13 of Akhenaten.[14] Possibly dating to Meryetaten's queenship may be some ring bezels from Amarna bearing her name, but as they lack a title, it cannot be certain that they date to her queenship, although the only other daughter so named is the likewise queenly Ankhesenpaaten.[15]

FIGURE 75 Block from Memphis, naming Smenkhkare and Meryetaten.

Apart from this material, Smenkhkare's most numerous memorials comprise further ring bezels and the molds for their manufacture, as well as some seal impressions.[16] But the most impressive is the vast brick-pillared structure which was added to the Great Palace in the center of Amarna. It was built at least in part with bricks stamped with what seems to be the building's name: "Ankhkheperure (in) the House of Rejoicing of the Aten."[17] This is often dubbed the "Coronation Hall" of Smenkhkare, but in fact no indication of its purpose survives.

There is no known unequivocal three-dimensional portrait of Smenkhkare, but a good case can be made for the middle coffin of Tutankhamun having been made for him (see further, pages 91–92, below). The face of the coffin (fig. 76, left) also resembles a facial reconstruction of the skull of what may be Smenkhkare's mummy (fig. 76, right: see just below). There are also a number of heads from house P47.2 that are similar to the visage revealed by these sources, and thus these may have been intended to depict Smenkhkare (e.g., fig. 77).

Smenkhkare's origins also remain a hotly debated topic. This is tied in with the question of the identity of the mummy found in KV55 in the Valley of the Kings which, on the basis of the inscriptions on the coffin that held it (from which the cartouches had been excised), was certainly intended in

FIGURE 76 a. Face of the middle coffin of Tutankhamun, probably originally made for Smenkhkare; from KV62 (Cairo JE60670). b. Reconstruction of the face of the mummy from KV55.

FIGURE 77 Plaster face which may represent Smenkhkare; from Amarna P.47.2 (Berlin ÄM21354).

its final form (cf. page 52) for a king of the Amarna Period, and thus can only be of him or Akhenaten himself. Crucial is the question of the age of the person at death, with the vast majority of assessments placing him in his (probably early) twenties,[18] although a handful have proposed something significantly older.[19] If the majority view is indeed correct,[20] the body cannot be that of Akhenaten, leaving Smenkhkare as the only candidate. The young age at death for Smenkhkare revealed by the KV55 mummy would rule out Akhenaten as the former's father—unless Smenkhkare had a significant independent reign after Akhenaten's death, a view not supported here. That Smenkhkare was a younger brother of Akhenaten has often been suggested, and this would be consistent with the DNA determination that gives the KV55 mummy the same genetics as the father of Tutankhamun, argued above (pages 47–48) to be Akhenaten.

But given this strong likelihood that Tutankhamun was indeed Akhenaten's son, why would the latter have raised his own younger brother to the coregency? The latter institution is generally seen as a mechanism for the "pre-accession" of the heir to the throne, and in this case Smenkhkare's promotion would be tantamount to setting aside Tutankhamun. However, while this seems to have been the basis for the institution when first seen during the Middle Kingdom, most provable later examples do *not* actually follow this pattern—for example, that of the female king Hatshepsut with her nephew Thutmose III.[21]

A clue may lie in the aforementioned rash of deaths within the royal family that should probably be dated around the time of Smenkhkare's appearance as coregent. One wonders whether Akhenaten, with his heir (Tutankhamun) only a child, was concerned about not only his personal mortality, but also the fate of his revolution if he too were carried off by the malady that had already claimed three of his children. In this context, appointing an adult younger brother as coruler would make sense, to ensure that there was no requirement for a regency (perhaps by those not committed to the Aten cult's perpetuation) in the event that Akhenaten died before Tutankhamun's majority. As an anointed king, Smenkhkare would simply continue to reign, but now with a different coruler—his young nephew Tutankhaten. Although, as just noted, arguments have been made that Smenkhkare survived Akhenaten and went on to have an independent reign, it seems most likely that he died after a fairly short period as coruler, perhaps another victim of the putative pestilence.

However, the "revolution guarantor" model seems soon to be resurrected, as Smenkhkare's passing appears to have marked the beginning of a further enhancement of Nefertiti's status, with the queen granted the right to wear the kingly blue crown. While it has been tentatively suggested that such headgear may be visible in one of the "durbar" scenes of Year 12,[22] she is certainly represented so crowned on an unfinished stela, dedicated by a man named Pay, showing her and Akhenaten seated together naked (fig. 78). Although the accompanying cartouches have never been filled in, the fact that only three of them were intended to label the two figures makes it clear that only one can be a fully fledged king. The other (whose gender is made clear by the shape of her breast) must be a "crowned queen."[23] The latter's identity with Nefertiti would seem difficult to doubt, especially as at least one of Nefertiti's statues had its distinctive flat-topped crown cut away and replaced by the blue crown (fig. 79).

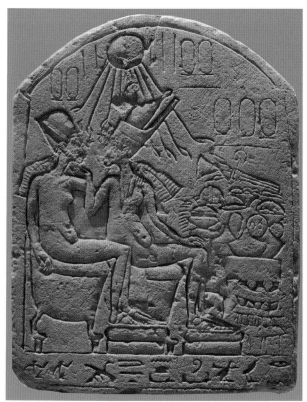

FIGURE 78 Unfinished stela dedicated by Pay, showing two naked figures wearing kingly crowns; the presence of only three royal cartouches, together with the physique of the left-hand figure, indicates that she must be a crowned queen (Berlin ÄM17813).

FIGURE 79 Head of statue, originally made for Nefertiti as a queen, but with the original crown cut away and replaced by a blue crown (Kestner 1970.49).

If Nefertiti was indeed taking over from Smenkhkare as "revolution guarantor," it is unclear why she was not at this time appointed full coregent. Perhaps there was some unease at such a promotion for someone who was not the actual offspring of a king, and that crowned queen was felt to be the furthest that things could be pushed. However, this would change during the last months of Akhenaten's life since, while on I *3ḫt* 15 of Akhenaten's Year 16 (a little more than a year before his death),[24] Nefertiti was still only King's Great Wife,[25] prior to her husband's death she had finally become a full king.

King Neferneferuaten

The Year 16 date was part of a routine graffito in a quarry at Deir Abu Hinnis, some ten kilometers north of Amarna (fig. 80). It records the extraction of stone for the *ḥwt-itn* (Small Aten Temple), and thus is an unequivocal statement of Nefertiti's formal status on that day. But a very different royal hierarchy is to be found on an inlaid box made at some point between then and Akhenaten's death (fig. 81).

FIGURE 80 Deir Abu Hinnis quarry 320 and its Year 16 graffito, naming Nefertiti as still King's Great Wife.

Discovered in the tomb of Tutankhamun, the box, which contained linen, had been broken, with the strip from the apex of the vaulted lid detached. The knobs at either end of this respectively bore the cartouches Ankhkheperure-mery-Neferkheperure and Neferneferuaten-mery-Waenre. "Ankhkheperure" had been the prenomen of Smenkhkare, and for a long time the names on the box were thought to be an alternate titulary for that king, but eventually were recognized as belonging to a separate monarch—eventually determined to have been a woman (see pages 128–29).

The concept of a woman as king goes back to at least the Middle Kingdom, although the historian Manetho, writing in Greek in the fourth century BC, alleges that under the third king of the Second Dynasty, "Binôthris" (that is, the king known in contemporary documents as Ninetjer), "it was decided that women might hold the kingly office." Moreover, a woman, Merneith, had apparently held supreme power during the First Dynasty, but without formal kingly titles and probably as a regent for an underage king,[26] but the first documented female king was not until Sobekneferu at the end of the Twelfth Dynasty (fig. 82).[27] The next was Hatshepsut, the best-documented of all such women,[28] who illustrates the gender fluidity to be seen in the way that such monarchs could be depicted and referred to. Sobekneferu had been shown wearing kingly headgear and with a pharaonic kilt worn over her typically female sheath dress, but Hatshepsut, although sometimes shown in female garb with just kingly headdress, was generally shown as though a man (fig. 83). In writing, Sobekneferu's titles always include the feminine *t*-suffix, but this is only irregularly found in those of Hatshepsut.

Neferneferuaten's known attestations lack the feminine suffix in her titles, but that suffix is found on occasion within her prenomen. Her cartouche names consistently incorporate epithets, the most common being those that call her "beloved" of one or another half of Akhenaten's prenomen. These half names stand where one would expect a god's name in pre- and post-Amarna kingly cartouches, re-emphasizing Akhenaten's

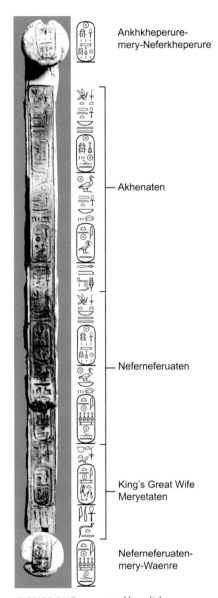

Ankhkheperure-mery-Neferkheperure

Akhenaten

Neferneferuaten

King's Great Wife Meryetaten

Neferneferuaten-mery-Waenre

FIGURE 81 Fragment of box lid from KV62, naming Akhenaten, Neferneferuaten, and Meryetaten (Cairo JE61500a).

FIGURE 82 Fragment of statue of Sobekneferu, shown wearing kingly regalia over normal female apparel (Louvre E27135).

status within the Atenist world view. In the case of the KV62 box, these are both used, split between her prenomen and nomen, but in some other cases only one is employed, in the prenomen, with a wholly different epithet, *3ḫt-n-ḥỉ.s*, "beneficial (fem.) for her husband," placed in the nomen. The full set of Neferneferuaten's known variant titularies run as follows:

A 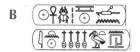 *ʿnḫ-ḫprw-rʿ-mry-nfr-ḫprw-rʿ*
nfr-nfrw-ỉtn-mry-wʿ-n-rʿ

B 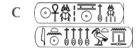 *ʿnḫ-ḫprw-rʿ-mry-wʿ-n-rʿ*
nfr-nfrw-ỉtn-3ḫt-n-ḥỉ.s

C *ʿnḫ-ḫprw-rʿ-mry-nfr-ḫprw-rʿ*
nfr-nfrw-ỉtn-3ḫt-n-ḥỉ.s

D  *ʿnḫ-ḫprw-rʿ-mry-ỉ[...]*
nfr-nfrw-ỉtn-mry-ỉ[mn?]

E 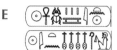 *ʿnḫ-ḫprw-rʿ-mry-ỉtn*
nfr-nfrw-ỉtn-ḥq3

FIGURE 83 King Hatshepsut shown (left) as a woman (RMO F 1928/9.2+MMA 29.3.3), (center) with a feminine body but male garb (MMA 29.3.2), and as a man (MMA 30.3.1); all from her memorial temple at Deir el-Bahari.

The identity of Neferneferuaten has been the subject of considerable debate since her first identification as a woman (pages 128–29, below) but, given that Nefertiti had borne the additional name Neferneferuaten since the early years of her husband's reign (page 26, above), since which time she had received exceptional honors (e.g., pages 13, 40, 61, above), and that she had already become a crowned queen, she must clearly be the leading candidate. Furthermore, Neferneferuaten's nomina in titularies B and C above cite a "husband" who can hardly be anyone other than the Akhenaten who is invoked in the associated prenomina. Accordingly, Nefertiti's identity with the king Neferneferuaten seems all but transparent.

This view is reinforced by the text on the strip between the two knobs on the KV62 box, which names Akhenaten, Neferneferuaten, and Queen Meryetaten, with Neferneferuaten in the place, between her husband and eldest daughter, where Nefertiti had stood canonically since the earliest days. The absence of Smenkhkare, in spite of the presence of his wife, reinforces the view that the latter was now a widow.

However, it seems clear that Meryetaten was not simply now a queen dowager. As is indicated by Rameses II's espousal of a number of his daughters as Great Wives after the deaths of his senior spouses, the need for someone to carry out the state and sacerdotal roles of the King's Great Wife was an enduring one. Thus, it seems likely that Meryetaten was now playing that role vis-à-vis her parents, emphasizing that "King's Wife" in the context was a role over and above that of simply a human spouse. Meryetaten may be fulfilling that role for her mother—presumably after her father's death—on another box lid from Tutankhamun's tomb, where Neferneferuaten's and Meryetaten's cartouches were later surcharged with those of Tutankhamun and Ankhesenamun.[29]

Probably dating to the brief period during which Akhenaten and Neferneferuaten were coregents are a set of three gilded faience bracelets, found in the tomb of Tutankhamun. One (probably originally one of a pair) bears the names of Akhenaten, and two those of Neferneferuaten.[30] At Amarna, at least some temple decoration seems to have been undertaken during the joint rule of Akhenaten and Neferneferuaten, as evidenced by a single block from Ashmunein, which preserves the latter's nomen cartouche, one border of her prenomen cartouche, and the remains of the titles and names of Ankhesenpaaten while yet a princess (fig. 84).[31] The latter suggests that it had been carved before Akhenaten's death, as it is argued below that Ankhesenpaaten transitioned to queen directly afterward (see page 83). A set of blocks from the same source, and coming from a pillar, with the same scene repeated in two sides, shows two kings, followed by a much smaller female (fig. 85).[32] Although associated blocks with the individuals' names have not yet been identified, it is most likely that they represent Akhenaten, Neferneferuaten, and Ankhesenpaaten, the latter owing to its size: as a queen, Meryetaten would presumably have been shown closer in size to the kings. It is also possible that the Tutankhuaten/

FIGURE 84 Block from Ashmunein naming Neferneferuaten and Ankhesenpaaten.

FIGURE 85 Blocks from Ashmunein showing two kings and a princess, most probably Akhenaten, Neferneferuaten, and Ankhesenpaaten.

FIGURE 86 The Great Gateway of the North Riverside Palace at Amarna.

Ankhesenpaaten pair of blocks (fig. 50) may also date from this phase.

There is no way of knowing whether two further monumental attestations of Neferneferuaten at Amarna should be placed before or after the death of Akhenaten. First, at the North Riverside Palace, the Great Gateway (fig. 86) was (re?)decorated after Neferneferuaten had become king. Here, the remains of at least two large-scale sets of cartouches survive, restorable to show that these were of variant C (fig. 87).[33] The variant B prenomen was also present among the fragments. Second, the house of the Master of Horse, Ranefer (N49.18—fig. 88),[34] was equipped with an inscribed limestone doorway bearing Neferneferuaten's variant A names and titles (fig. 89),[35] as part of the house's rebuilding from an earlier incarnation.[36] A "late" date for the city neighborhood in question may be suggested by the finding of a ring bezel of Smenkhkare in a nearby house (N49.19).[37]

A stela, one of whose fragments was found in the so-called North Harem of the Great Palace, was reworked to change the single cartouche of Nefertiti into the double cartouches of Neferneferuaten. However, its present state makes it difficult to know what concomitant changes were made to the scene it once bore (fig. 90).[38] Neferneferuaten is also named on various ring

FIGURE 87 Plaster from the Great Gateway of the North Riverside Palace naming Neferneferuaten, with restoration of cartouche inset (Liverpool 1973.1.545a).

FIGURE 88 The house of Ranefer (N49.18) at Amarna, rebuilt during the reign of Neferneferuaten.

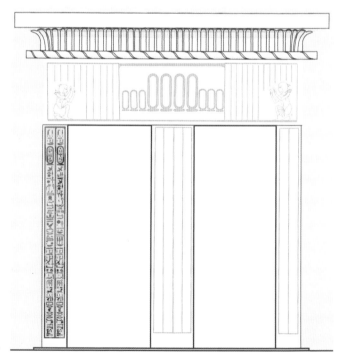

FIGURE 89 Reconstruction of the doorway of the house of Ranefer, including texts mentioning Neferneferuaten.

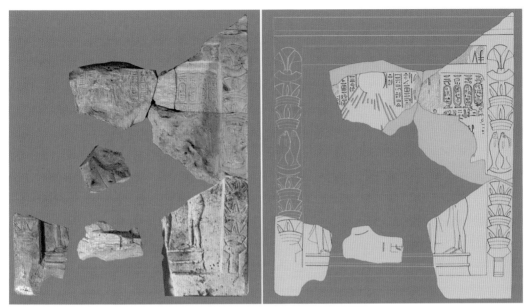

FIGURE 90 Fragmentary stela, modified after Neferneferuaten's appointment as coregent (Petrie UC410 + Cairo JE64959).

bezels in[39] and around[40] the Great Palace and houses T36.5 and T36.55.[41] Interestingly, in the Workmen's Village, only a small proportion of the royal names are those of Akhenaten; a larger number name Neferneferuaten, Smenkhkare a few more, the largest group naming Tutankhaten/amun.[42]

After Akhenaten

As noted above, Nefertiti's elevation to kingship as Neferneferuaten could have come at most fifteen months before Akhenaten's death, and probably significantly less. Given the apparent reluctance to give her full kingship straight after Smenkhkare's death, one assumes that some crisis pushed Akhenaten into taking the final step, but whether this was one of health or political threats is unknown. Given the upheavals that Akhenaten had imposed on key components of Egyptian society, he will clearly have had many enemies. It is quite possible that these coalesced into a genuine threat to the king—and may indeed have ended his life.

What happened immediately after the king's death—whether natural or otherwise—has been much debated. There have been suggestions that it was at this point that, as related in a Hittite text, a king's childless widow (she is referred to in this text as *dakhamunzu*, a transparent transcription of the Egyptian *t3-ḥmt-nsw*, "the king's wife") wrote to Shuppiluliuma, king of the Hittites. She requested that a son of his be sent to Egypt,

whom she would marry and make king.[43] This event has usually been placed at the end of Tutankhamun's reign, which would fit with the writing of the dead king's name (prenomen) in the Hittite text, but others have argued that it should be placed at the end of the reign of Akhenaten, the name being corrupt, and that the Egyptian protagonist was actually Nefertiti.

However, the text is explicit in stating that the queen in question had no son—yet as we have argued above, Tutankhaten was most likely Nefertiti's son. Even if he was not, Tutankhaten was certainly a king's son, and thus not lightly set aside in favor of a foreigner. Also, on our reconstruction, Nefertiti was now no mere King's Wife, as was the Hittites' correspondent at the time of Akhenaten's demise, but a full king. The whole scenario is sufficiently contrary to that seen in the Hittite sources to make it unlikely that the former Nefertiti was involved, and that the conventional attribution to a decade later remains far more credible.[44]

In any case, Neferneferuaten's reign certainly continued beyond her husband's death, as shown by a graffito dated to III *3ḫt* 10 of Year 3 of Ankhkheperure-mery-A[. . .] Neferneferuaten-mery-A[. . .] (fig. 91).[45] Both epithets were partly lost when the graffito was first copied and are now entirely gone (fig. 92), and there is nothing to help further restore the first one. On the other hand, the example within the nomen could credibly be restored as "mery-Amun"—beloved of Amun! That the former Nefertiti could, so soon after her husband's death, be reconciled to the deity whom he had devoted so much effort to suppressing would indeed be surprising. Such a restoration would accordingly have seemed unlikely, were it not for the contents of the graffito itself.

The tomb chapel in which the graffito was written dates to the time of Amenhotep III (or conceivably Thutmose IV). Its choice by the scribe in question seems to have no obvious significance, other than it being an easily accessible place, low on the Sheikh Abd el-Qurna hill (fig. 93). But the key point is that it comprises a prayer to *Amun* by "the *w'b*-priest and Scribe of Divine Offerings of Amun . . . Pawah, son of Itefseneb," showing not only that the god was no longer proscribed, but that priests of the god were once again operating openly.

FIGURE 92 Current state of the dateline of the TT139 graffito.

FIGURE 93 The Sheikh Abd el-Qurna hill, showing the location of TT139.

A further interesting point about the graffito is that Pawah—who was blind—and his brother, the Outline Draftsman Batjay, who actually wrote it on his sibling's behalf, were both employed in the "ḥwt of Ankhkheperure at Thebes." Ḥwt + royal name is well attested as a designation of a memorial temple founded by or for the king in question,[46] all certain examples of which were on the west bank at Thebes. The key question here is to which "Ankhkheperure" this sanctuary belonged. Given that the graffito is dated to the reign of a king with a "core" prenomen of Ankhkheperure, one might at first sight assume that the temple was hers, built rapidly in view of the fact that clergy were already in place, not just artisans such as the Outline Draftsman Batjay.

However, it is clear that, although sharing the basic "Ankhkheperure" core prenomen, in all other contexts Smenkhkare invariably used the simple form "Ankhkheperure," while Neferneferuaten always employed "Ankhkheperure + EPITHET." Throughout the graffito, the temple is always of a simple "Ankhkheperure," the prima facie identification of the owner of the temple being accordingly Smenkhkare.[47] This of course raises all kinds of questions, given that Smenkhkare seems to have died at the height of the Amarna revolution, and thus his possession of a Theban mortuary establishment, especially one in which an Amun cult existed a few years later, seems strange. On the other hand, as discussed above (pages 54–55), the active persecution of Amun may have only taken place fairly late in Akhenaten's reign—perhaps even only after Smenkhkare's death—meaning that Smenkhkare may have been able to found such an establishment without any particular issues, even if little work was actually done on it before his demise. Clearly, during the persecution it cannot have functioned, but following Akhenaten's death it could have been brought back into use or, indeed, inaugurated for the first time.

While we clearly have this "Year 3" associated with Neferneferuaten, it is by no means certain how we should interpret it. Egyptian kings usually counted regnal years from their accession, whether as sole king or as coregent,[48] so this could represent three years from Neferneferuaten's appointment during the last year of Akhenaten's reign. On the other hand, Hatshepsut simply used the regnal years of Thutmose III, in spite of not becoming a king until his Year 7, while Tawosret continued the year numbering of her late ward, Siptah. It is interesting that both these cases involved women in a "nonstandard" context, and their model may also be applicable to Neferneferuaten.

As already suggested, the appointments of Smenkhkare and Neferneferuaten to coregency should probably be seen as "nonstandard," as means of guaranteeing the accession of the underage Tutankhamun without the need for a third-party regency. In this case, when Akhenaten died, Neferneferuaten would have transitioned from being her husband's coregent to being that of the new king, her son Tutankhamun. While some have argued that the latter did not become king until after Neferneferuaten's demise, it is difficult to conceive of a scenario where the legitimately born heir to the throne would be set aside in favor of his nonroyally-born mother, whose accession had clearly occurred at the direction of his father.[49]

On that basis, it may have been that the "Year 3" of the TT139 graffito represents a year count begun at the accession of Tutankhamun that was also used by Neferneferuaten. While there is no proof of such an arrangement, such as any material naming or showing the two pharaohs together, very little has in any case survived from the earliest part of Tutankhamun's reign, while the posthumous fate of Neferneferuaten (pages 90–94, below) may have included the destruction of relevant material. Thus, a working hypothesis for the chronology of the period would seem to be as follows:

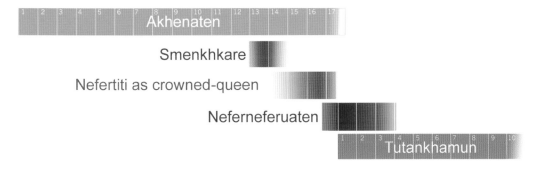

Tutankhaten

At the time of his accession, the new king still bore his birth name. He seems to have been married from the outset to his sister Ankhesenpaaten, the royal couple being respectively probably around eight and eleven years old. Among the young king's first acts would have been to carry out Akhenaten's burial, the proper interment of one's predecessor being seemingly one of the requirements for royal succession.[50]

As previously noted, the Royal Tomb at Amarna had already received the mummies of Queen Tiye and Princesses Meketaten, Neferneferure, and Setepenre, and may also have been the burial place of Smenkhkare, on the basis of his death occurring while he was still coregent. Now, Akhenaten's body would have been placed in the main burial chamber of the sepulcher (fig. 94)—which already held the burial of his mother, Tiye—within the sarcophagus that had been made with its corners embraced by Nefertiti (fig. 35), who was now one of his principal mourners.

That Atenism remained for the moment dominant is indicated by the decoration of the throne that was presumably made early in the reign, showing Tutankhaten and Ankhesenpaaten in a mode characteristic of their parents (figs. 95, 96).[51] However, a small stela, apparently from Amarna, showed Tutankhaten making offerings to Amun

FIGURE 94 The main burial chamber of the Royal Tomb at Amarna (TA26), which held the burials of at least Akhenaten and Tiye.

FIGURE 95 Right side of the throne from KV62, showing the unaltered nomen of Tutankhaten (Cairo JE62028).

and Mut (fig. 97) and, together with the mention of a "live" cult of Amun in the TT139 graffito, implies a rapid reversal of the proscription of Amun that, whichever reconstruction of the years directly following the death of Akhenaten one prefers, must clearly have been decided by Neferneferuaten.

This reversal of a policy that had been so important to her late husband is most striking, especially in view of Nefertiti's previous intimate role within the Aten cult. However, history is replete with examples of dramatic reversals of principles in the face of reality and, particularly if Akhenaten's demise had been other than natural, Neferneferuaten may have been confronted with hard choices in the weeks following the death of her husband. Her own safety and that of the

FIGURE 96 Scene from the front of the throne, showing the king and queen, in this case with their names changed to their Amun forms.

young king and queen may well have been issues, although it is also possible that her own personal beliefs may have actually been less extreme than those of Akhenaten, and she may in any case have been favorable to the religious cohabitation that seems to have existed during the earlier part of his reign.

We accordingly see during the three years following the death of Akhenaten an attempted "triangulation" between the old and the new: the capital remained at Amarna, and the kings and queen retained their Aten-citing names, but Amun was unproscribed,

FIGURE 97 Stela of Tutankhaten, showing him offering to Amun and Mut; apparently from Amarna (Berlin ÄM14197).

and resources were again released to cults beyond that of the Aten. Something like the latter is described in a stela from Karnak (fig. 98).

> Now when His Majesty arose as king the temples and the estates of the gods and goddesses from Elephantine to the marshes of the Delta had fallen into ruin [. . .]. Their shrines had fallen down and turned into ruin—fields overgrown with weeds, their sanctuaries were as if they had never been. Their temples had become footpaths. The land was in confusion and the gods had turned their backs on this land. If an [army was] sent to Syria to extend the frontiers of Egypt, it had no success. If you asked a god for advice, he would not attend; and if one spoke to a goddess likewise she would not attend. Hearts were faint in bodies because everything that had been, was destroyed.

It then goes on to describe

> rebuilding [the gods'] sanctuaries as his monuments for ever and eternity, endowing them with offerings forever, supplying them with divine offerings daily, laying aside bread from the earth. He added to that which had existed before, doing more than his predecessors had ever done.

The stela was solely in the name of the king, shown accompanied only by his wife in the lunette, but its year date is broken away. Any clue derived from the forms of their names has been lost by the stela's later usurpation by Horemheb, who surcharged Tutankhamun's cartouches and erased his wife's name and figures. Thus, it is unclear whether this represents work directed by Neferneferuaten but for political reasons credited solely to Tutankhamun in a stela erected contemporaneously, a later commemoration of this work, or a fresh round of restoration begun after Neferneferuaten's demise.[52]

That Amarna was intended to remain—for the time being, at least—the capital is suggested by a number of factors. First, there is the considerable number of named ring bezels of both Neferneferuaten and Tutankhamun found there; second, we have the aforementioned decoration of the gateways of the North Riverside Palace and the house of Ranefer incorporating Neferneferuaten's names; and third, it seems clear that the royal necropolis was planned to remain there. Although the Royal Tomb (TA26) was presumably permanently closed after Akhenaten's interment there, two additional large tombs of undoubtedly royal type were begun nearby (fig. 99: see further just below).[53]

FIGURE 98 Restoration stela of Tutankhamun, later usurped by Horemheb; from Karnak (Cairo CG34183).

FIGURE 99 The side wadi of the Royal Wadi at Amarna containing tombs TA28 and 29.

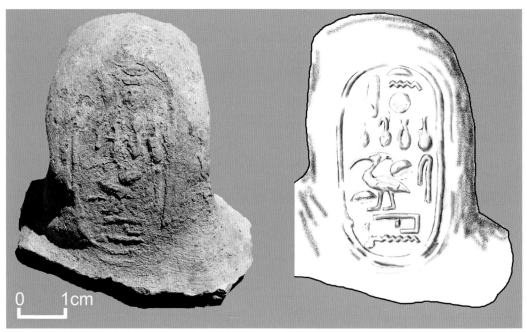

FIGURE 100 Jar handle with nomen of Neferneferuaten from Tell el-Borg.

Beyond the limited amount of material at Amarna and Thebes, the reign of Neferneferuaten also left traces in northern Sinai. Here, at the fortress of Tell el-Borg (fig. 100), stamped jar handles with both the prenomen and nomen of Neferneferuaten were found, as were two bearing the prenomen of Tutankhamun.[54] These clearly indicate activity at the fort under these rulers, although the sealings were found too dispersed to have any bearing on whether they might have been reigning together at the time. The site also revealed sealings of Akhenaten, Ay, and Horemheb. They show that the fort was in continual occupation throughout the late Eighteenth Dynasty, and probably had been since the time of Thutmose III.

Royal Tombs

One of the aforementioned sepulchers at Amarna, TA29, had penetrated some forty-five meters into the mountain before being abandoned. It may have been begun for Smenkhkare, and then continued for Nefertiti, as crowned queen and/or as Neferneferuaten (fig. 101, left). The other, TA27, was less far advanced when abandoned, and was accordingly most likely intended for Tutankhaten (fig. 101, right).

Like any other Egyptian king, Neferneferuaten began to collect together her funerary equipment during her lifetime. As queen, she would have previously done likewise, and two unprovenanced shabti fragments of Nefertiti as a royal wife are known (fig. 102).[55]

FIGURE 101 Left: TA29, possibly the tomb intended for Neferneferuaten; right: TA27, possibly intended for Tutankhaten.

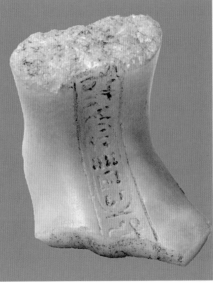

FIGURE 102 Two shabti fragments of Nefertiti (left: Louvre AF9904; right: Brooklyn 33.51).

Their existence has been argued as indicating that Nefertiti had died as a queen,[56] but since there is no reason why such items could not have been made in anticipation of death, like the rest of any person's burial outfit, this cannot be sustained.

In addition to such "core" material as shabtis, the sarcophagus, coffins, and canopic equipment, high-status tombs of the New Kingdom contained many more items as compared to other periods.[57] In particular, in kingly tombs, figures of the king and various

FIGURE 103 Funerary figure of Neferneferuaten on a panther, reused in KV62 (Cairo JE60714).

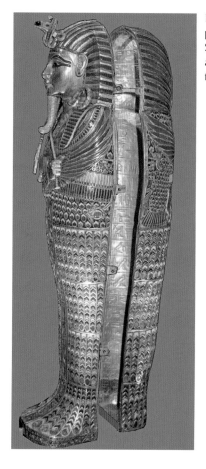

FIGURE 104 Canopic coffinette, probably originally made for Smenkhkare and successively appropriated for Tutankhamun; from KV62 (Cairo JE60688).

funerary deities, to be placed in shrines in the tomb, were an important feature, with fragments surviving in some of even the most heavily robbed royal sepulchers.[58] At least one such figure made for Neferneferuaten survives (fig. 103), uninscribed as such but unmistakable by its combination of a White Crown with an obviously female physique.

However, this piece was found integrated into the equipment of the tomb of Tutankhamun, paired with a very similar, but clearly male and slightly differently made, figure;[59] both pieces bore Tutankhamun's name in paint. Similarly, a wide range of other pieces made for Neferneferuaten and identifiable by their original inscriptions were found in Tutankhamun's sepulcher, along with others whose style or other factors raise strong suspicions as to their intended owner.[60]

FIGURE 105 The mummy trappings of Tutankhamun; some of the side elements were originally made for Neferneferuaten; from KV62 (Cairo JE61903+60673).

Among the most striking of the first category are the gold, glass-inlaid coffinettes that contained Tutankhamun's mummified viscera (fig. 104). Inside these, Neferneferuaten's names remain as readable palimpsests under those of Tutankhamun. Also intimately linked with the body were parts of the golden trappings that adorned Tutankhamun's mummy (fig. 105). These had come from a similar network made for Neferneferuaten, as had parts of the straps that suspended the pendant scarab that also formed part of these trappings. Beyond these, there was at least one pectoral (fig. 106)[61] and a ceremonial bow[62] on which the names of Neferneferuaten had been replaced by those of Tutankhamun (and which Neferneferuaten may have taken over from a previous owner), plus the aforementioned box of Neferneferuaten and Meryetaten, taken over for Tutankhamun and Ankhesenamun.

In addition to these items that had definitely belonged to Neferneferuaten before being reworked for Tutankhamun are a number where suspicions have been raised. The middle of the nest of three coffins employed for his burial (fig. 107) looks to have been

made as a set with the canopic coffinettes, both in its decorative scheme and in the form
of the face (fig. 76, left), which is certainly not that found on the other coffins, nor in
other representations of Tutankhamun. There are no gross signs of names being changed,
but the cartouches could easily have been switched in their entirety, as was the case with
those on the fronts of the coffinettes; however, those on the inside were chased into the
gold, making it very difficult to rework without leaving traces.[63]

What is interesting about both the coffinettes and the coffin is that the face is *not*
consistent with that of Nefertiti—nor any of the (female) candidates who have been
suggested for Neferneferuaten's previous identity. Rather, it appears distinctly male and,
as already noted (page 69, above), is consistent with both certain plaster heads from
Amarna and a facial reconstruction of what seems to be Smenkhkare's mummy. Thus
it would appear that for Tutankhamun these items were third-hand, having been made
for Smenkhkare, not employed for his burial,[64] and then taken over by Neferneferuaten
as part of her own burial outfit. There are no signs of Smenkhkare's names in the
coffinettes,[65] but they (like the coffin) may have been made with undecorated interiors
and inscribed within only when taken over by Neferneferuaten. Externally, usurpation
only required excision and replacement of one gold-and-glass-inlaid cartouche: while it
is clear that this has been done, it is impossible to judge how many times.

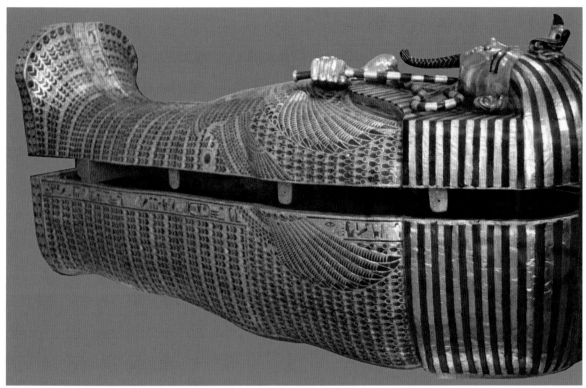

FIGURE 107 Gilded and glass-inlaid coffin that was ultimately employed as the middle element of Tutankhamun's coffin nest, but seems to have been made for Smenkhkare and appropriated in the interim for Neferneferuaten; from KV62 (Cairo JE60670).

Another item that may at one point have belonged to Neferneferuaten is Tutankhamun's sarcophagus, which shows undoubted traces of major rework, but whether this was a result of it having been taken over from Neferneferuaten or was required by the change of name from Tutankhaten to -amun (with a much larger nomen cartouche) is a moot point.[66] The second- and third-innermost of the nest of shrines surrounding the sarcophagus also show signs of having had cartouches replaced, as well as including royal epithets more appropriate to Akhenaten (and possibly his corulers) than Tutankhamun himself.[67] But it is not impossible that these changes were linked to Tutankhamun's change of nomen, rather than an indication of original ownership by an earlier monarch, for example Neferneferuaten.[68]

A further group of material potentially reworked for Tutankhamun are some of his large shabtis. None show any gross signs of rework, and even the "presentation" examples explicitly made as burial gifts for the king have noticeably swelling hips. Nevertheless, some (e.g., fig. 108) have a body shape that seems to go beyond the rest, and could potentially be seen as having started life as part of Neferneferuaten's equipment—especially as their faces also diverge from the range seen across most of the group.

FIGURE 108 Two shabtis of Tutankhamun; their body shapes and facial features suggest that they might originally have been commissioned for Neferneferuaten; from KV62 (Cairo JE60821, JE60824b).

The Death of Neferneferuaten

Neferneferuaten's only dated document is the Year 3 graffito discussed above. That her tenure of the throne ended in a bad way is strongly suggested by the fact that her kingly funerary equipment was never employed for her, but was reallocated to Tutankhamun, indicating that she was not buried as a king. Furthermore, if the identification of the mummy of the Younger Lady from KV35 is indeed correct, her death will have been horrific.

Much of the left side of the mummy's face has been broken away (fig. 109, left). While most earlier assumptions had been that this, like other damage to the body, had been the result of the depredations of tomb robbers,[69] CT study[70] now "suggests that the injury . . . was likely inflicted before mummification took place . . . more likely inflicted by hitting the face with a heavy object . . . caus[ing] severe shock and bleeding." While accident cannot be ruled out (for example, a strong kick by an animal), the aforementioned posthumous treatment of Neferneferuaten gives rise to strong suspicions of foul play. The CT study also suggested an age at death of between twenty-five and thirty-five years, the upper end of which would be consistent with Nefertiti having been married to Akhenaten around her mid-teens and dying almost exactly two decades later, shortly after Neferneferuaten's Year 3.

FIGURE 109 The head of the Younger Lady from KV35 (Cairo CG61072) and a facial reconstruction by Elisabeth Daynès.

The circumstances surrounding what may have been the murder of Neferneferuaten are of course unknowable in the absence of anything other than the circumstantial evidence of the mummy and the posthumous disregard indicated by the release of her funerary equipment for recycling. However, there is a strong likelihood that the policy of "triangulation" between the Aten and the traditional cults may have been insufficient for those who wished to see a full repudiation of Akhenaten's religious experiment, to which end the removal of Neferneferuaten and the institution of a regency of more appropriately minded people would be necessary. Or might Neferneferuaten have been viewed by die-hard supporters of Akhenaten's revolution as a traitor to her late husband's cause and thus her death aimed at a new regime that would reinvigorate the revolution?

In the event, the new regime would be one of full-scale counter-reformation, in the persons of Neferneferuaten's probable father, Ay, and brother-in-law, Horemheb. But while it is not impossible that Ay could have plotted, or at least acquiesced to, his daughter's assassination, there are many examples in history of a plot being successful in its primary objective of killing a leader but less so in replacing them with the plotters themselves or their agents (for example, the "harem conspiracy" that killed Rameses III[71]). Thus, at this distance, one can but attribute Neferneferuaten's death to "person or persons unknown."

4 LIMBO

As already noted, following Neferneferuaten's death, Horemheb, who became formal regent, and Ay, who seemingly held no official role (apart from what seems to have been an honorary vizierate) but was perhaps the more pivotal figure,[1] pursued a clear policy of decisive movement away from any retention of Atenism as part of the emerging settlement. The young king and queen both had their names switched to Amun-citing forms and the restoration of monuments pushed forward apace. In addition, the first moves were made to start dismantling Akhenaten's work at Karnak. This included a number of sphinxes originally representing Akhenaten and Nefertiti being decapitated and given new rams' heads, plus small figures of Tutankhamun in front of their chests. They were then used to line the processional route between the Karnak precincts of Amun and Mut.[2] Some of the stone used for Tutankhamun's memorial temple was also scavenged from Aten structures.

It also seems to have been from this point that Amarna was abandoned as a capital city, there being only one ring bezel and a mold apparently attesting to activity by the king at the site after his change of name,[3] with a return of civil administration to Memphis, while Thebes resumed its role as principal national religious center. On the other hand, there is likely to have been a continued, if steadily diminishing, official presence at Amarna until as late as the reign of Horemheb.[4]

The Burial Place of Neferneferuaten

In view of the run-down of Amarna, an issue will have been what to do with the high-status bodies interred there. Maintaining security would have been problematic, leaving aside any ritual concerns that may have also been significant. Accordingly, the Royal Tomb was

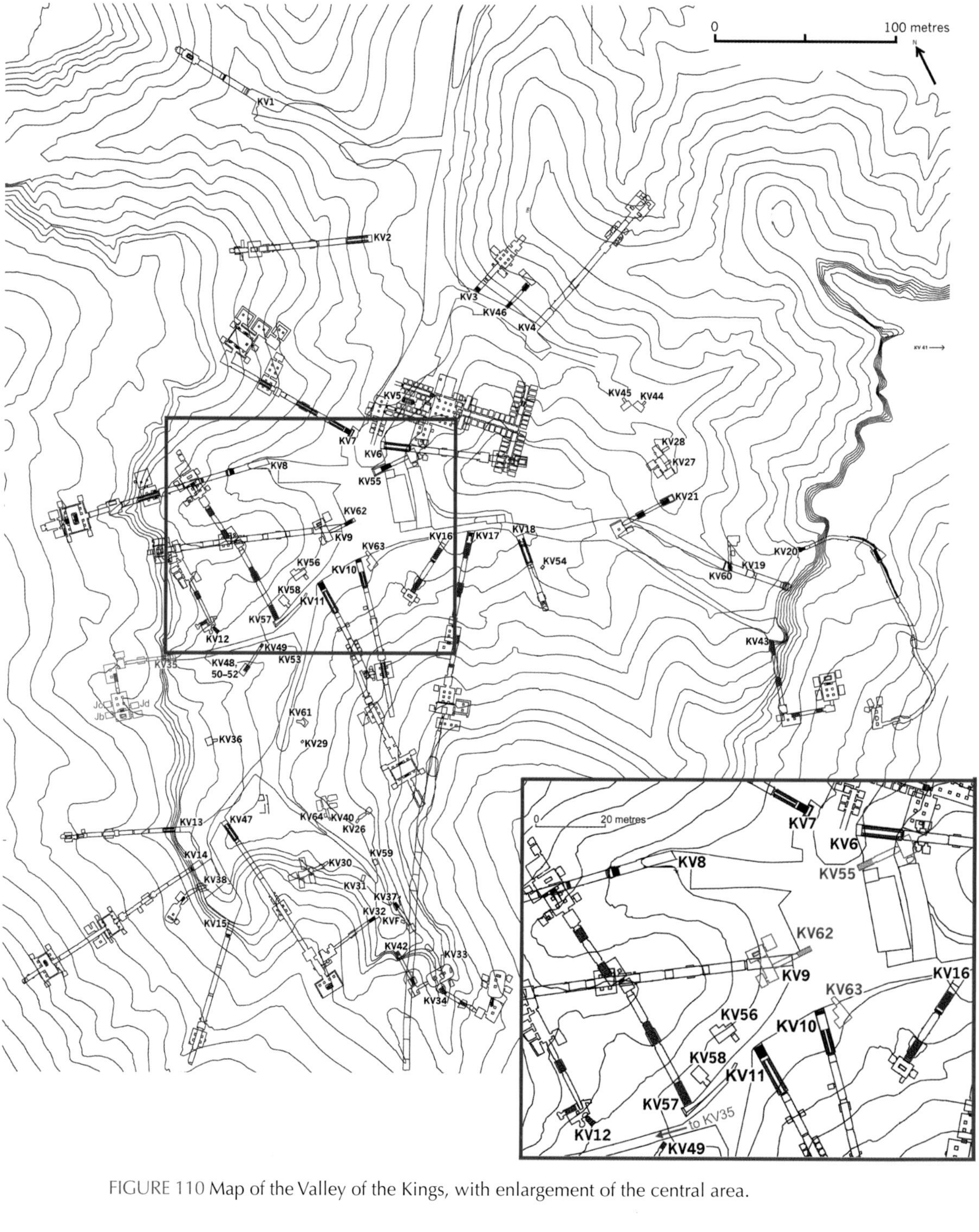

FIGURE 110 Map of the Valley of the Kings, with enlargement of the central area.

FIGURE 111 The central area of the Valley of the Kings.

probably ordered emptied not long after the decision to leave Amarna was taken, for reburial in the ancestral cemetery of the Valley of the Kings at Thebes (fig. 110). It is likely that the question of the disposal of Neferneferuaten's body was tied into this process.

At this point, the Royal Tomb probably held six bodies, those of Akhenaten, Smenkhkare, Tiye, Meketaten, Neferneferure, and Setepenre. The first three appear to have been deposited in KV55 in the center of the Valley of the Kings (fig. 111), as evidenced by surviving magic bricks of Akhenaten, a funerary shrine of Tiye, and the coffin and body of Smenkhkare.[5] Mummification materials from all the burials in the Royal Tomb may be the source of the "embalmers' cache" placed in the nearby shaft tomb KV63.[6] As for the three princesses, nothing is yet known of their destination, but a hitherto unknown tomb in the same area of the Valley of the Kings—an area in which Tutankhamun would also be buried—would seem most likely. Certainly, there is enough space in the part of this area that remains unexcavated to accommodate such a sepulcher, and provisional remote-sensing results include a potential echo halfway between KV55 and KV62,[7] and another directly north of KV62 (page 131, below). If the move of the bodies from Amarna took place soon after Neferneferuaten's death, might this putative tomb have been an ideal burial place for her, alongside her daughters?

FIGURE 112 North wall of the burial chamber of KV62.

There are, however, other options—not excluding KV55. While there is no direct evidence that the Younger Lady was ever in KV55, she was found in KV35 lying next to an "Elder Lady," identified on DNA grounds and through hair sample comparison as Queen Tiye. Given the presence of Tiye's funerary shine in KV55, it seems clear that Tiye was originally an occupant of KV55: might the Elder and Younger Ladies have been moved together from KV55 to KV35? Or might KV62, ultimately the tomb of Tutankhamun, have been Neferneferuaten's resting place, from which she was moved when the sepulcher was requisitioned for Tutankhamun's funeral—which was when the removal of Tiye from KV55 seems to have taken place (page 101)?

The idea that KV62 might have originated as Neferneferuaten's tomb has generated a number of elaborate theories. One of these in particular, based on what proved to be erroneous scans of the walls of the burial chamber (see page 131, below), suggested that she lay undisturbed in a hitherto undiscovered set of inner chambers, Tutankhamun having merely usurped the outer part of the tomb and sealed off the rest.[8] This scheme also proposed that the paintings on the north wall of the KV62 burial chamber (fig. 112) had been originally painted for Neferneferuaten and were subsequently modified for Tutankhamun. This was based in part on the fact that they had been executed to a different canon of proportions than those on the other three,[9] to somewhat different technical standards, and originally with a white background. The latter had subsequently been repainted yellow to match the others.[10] In this scenario, Tutankhamun's name would have replaced that of Neferneferuaten and Ay's that of Tutankhamun.[11]

On the other hand, given that Neferneferuaten's burial seems to have omitted all material made for her as king, it would argue against burial in a room showing the funeral of a pharaoh. Rather, it would suggest a very basic interment, perhaps utilizing some material that had been made when she had been no more than a queen, with no attempt (or need) to provide kingly decoration in the place she was laid to rest.[12] Thus, if KV62 was indeed where Neferneferuaten was buried, all that would have been needed when the tomb was taken over for Tutankhamun was for her coffined mummy and any accompanying material to be removed from what was at the time an undecorated single-chambered tomb. This would then have been extended and decorated for Tutankhamun.

Wherever Neferneferuaten was actually initially buried, and assuming that it was indeed in the central area of the Valley, it seems likely that she was moved during the period directly following Tutankhamun's burial in KV62. It is now known that the whole area (including KV55, KV62, KV63, and any undiscovered tomb) was sealed under a thick layer of flood debris very shortly after Tutankhamun's funeral (and the abortive robbery of the tomb that took place directly afterward).[13] Thus any moves cannot have taken place after this point in time.

The moves we know about were from KV55, where the mummies of Akhenaten and Tiye were removed entirely, leaving behind only two of the former's magic bricks and the latter's dismantled shrine. This was seemingly intended to accompany her mummy out of the tomb, but the first panel jammed in the entrance corridor, meaning that the operation had to be abandoned.[14] Smenkhkare was left behind, but with his coffin and canopic jars deprived of his names, an act that indicates that the moves out of the tomb were at the head of a broader program that would soon see the Amarna rulers written out of history. This would, ironically, come to also include Ay, who was probably one of the orchestrators of the scheme at its beginning.

Nothing is known of the fate of Akhenaten's mummy, but had the intention been to just deprive it of its identity, it would surely have been left in KV55 and treated in the same way as Smenkhkare. One can only thus assume that its fate was destruction, perhaps by fire, the most horrific fate possible for a dead person in Egyptian belief. Tiye's mummy's initial destination is debatable. There is some evidence to suggest that it may have been moved to her husband's tomb, WV22, in the West Valley,[15] but this is equivocal, and its remoteness from KV55 might suggest somewhere closer—in particular KV35, where the Elder Lady ultimately ended up alongside the Younger Lady.

That the Elder Lady had *not* come there from WV22 with Amenhotep III when he was placed in the tomb's chamber Jb (see fig. 110), along with seven other kings and one woman, in Twentieth or Twenty-first Dynasty times is suggested by the fact that these mummies seem to have remained essentially untouched after their arrival in KV35.[16] On

FIGURE 113 Chamber Jc of KV35 as found.

the contrary, the Elder and Younger Ladies were found in a different chamber (Jc), having been robbed of their coffins and wrappings and left on the floor (fig. 113). Alongside them was found the likewise naked mummy of a young male that seems to have come from chamber Jd, where he had probably been buried during the reign of Amenhotep II.[17] Accordingly, it would seem that they had been in the tomb when it was first robbed, probably in late Rameside times, an occasion when the tomb's owner, Amenhotep II, seemingly lost his coffins as well, although in his case a replacement was provided later, probably when the Jb mummies were installed.[18]

The two ladies' mummies would thus seem to have been in the tomb before the great shifting of royal mummies that appears to have begun at the end of the Twentieth Dynasty. Accordingly, the most likely scenario seems to be that they were moved directly to KV35 on their extraction from their previous places of interment around the time of Tutankhamun's burial. This would be consistent with any of the options noted above for Neferneferuaten's burial; in the present state of knowledge it is difficult to choose between them.

Oblivion

As already noted, the removal of Neferneferuaten from her first tomb was simply one act in a process that was intended to consign her whole family to eternal obscurity. Under Tutankhamun, the dismantling of Akhenaten's monuments was likely prompted by a desire to reuse materials from buildings that were no longer wanted. However, over the coming years, such reuse was often accompanied by the erasure of names—now extended to Tutankhamun and Ay. It was presumably during the late Eighteenth or early Nineteenth Dynasty that most of the images of Akhenaten and Nefertiti (and others, but not generally the daughters), were mutilated (fig. 114). Their cartouches, and often those of the Aten as well, were also attacked, although there were of course oversights (for example, fig. 115). In any case, blocks from the Amarna temples were shipped across the river to Ashmunein as filling for the temple pylons being built there by Rameses II, while those from the Aten complex at Karnak had suffered a similar fate under Horemheb, who used them within Karnak Pylons II, IX, and X.

FIGURE 114 Scene of the royal family in the tomb chapel of Meryre i (TA4), showing the mutilation of the faces and the cartouches of the king, the queen, and the Aten.

FIGURE 115 Cartouches of the god, king, and queen inadvertently left intact on the inner front lintel of the tomb chapel of Panehsy (TA6).

By the time that the lists of kings of Egypt were compiled on the walls of the temples of Sethy I and Rameses II at Abydos, the "official" royal succession jumped straight from Amenhotep III to Horemheb (fig. 117). In an account of a long-running legal case composed under Rameses II, the aggregate years from Akhenaten's accession to the death of Ay had been incorporated into the reign of Horemheb (fig. 116).[19] The whole family had thus apparently passed into oblivion.

Yet nearly a millennium later, when Manetho (page 73, above) came to compose his list of Egyptian kings, although he conformed to the early Nineteenth Dynasty canon by following his "Amenôphis" (= Amenhotep III) with "Ôrus" (= Horemheb), he then listed the following:[20]

> Acenchêrês ("his daughter")
> Rathôtis ("her brother")
> Acenchêrês ("his son")
> Acenchêrês II ("his son")
> Harmaïs ("his son")

"Harmaïs" would seem to be a dittography of Horemheb, while the others clearly represent a garbled, misordered remembrance of the Amarna kings. Most interesting is the recognition of there having been a female ruler during the period, with "Acenchêrês" a passable potential rendering of "Ankhkheperure," as well as potential distortion of "Akhenaten." One king is missing, presumably the ephemeral Smenkhkare, in spite of the potential for more than one "Acenchêrês," and it is unclear how Tutankhamun and Ay became "Rathôtis" and an "Acenchêrês" (presumably this way around). However, the key point here is that, in spite of the early attempt to erase them from history, even in Ptolemaic times there was enough material for Manetho to be aware that there were kings in the period other than the canonical Amenhotep III and Horemheb—including a woman—and to make some attempt at listing them.

But even if some fragmentary records endured into Hellenistic times, those relating to Nefertiti and her family would share the same utter eclipse as those of more enduring historical figures. A burgeoning Christianity replaced the old faiths and pushed the millennia-old hieroglyphic writing system and its cursive derivatives into obsolescence. By the time that the Edict of Theodosius in AD 393 closed the last remaining pagan temples in Egypt, pharaonic Egypt had become all but a closed book in its own terms. For over a thousand years, anyone seeking knowledge of it was restricted to the garbled material deriving from the classical sources and the Bible. It would not be until the beginning of the nineteenth century that it once again became possible to engage meaningfully with the remains still surviving from ancient Egypt, and begin to draw back the veil that had for so long hidden its inhabitants from modern view.

FIGURE 116 Block from the Inscription of Mose, with its attribution of a Year 59 to Horemheb highlighted.

5 RESURRECTION

uring the first part of the nineteenth century, the study of ancient Egypt was transformed by the availability of reasonably accurate records of standing monuments and the significant number of objects that were finding their ways into European museums. Many were as a result of the French expedition to Egypt in 1798 and the collecting activities of the European consuls-general in Egypt during the 1810s and 1820s.[1] The latter decade saw the key steps forward, particularly when hieroglyphs began to once again be readable, for the first time in some 1,500 years.

Although it would be decades before running texts could be read with relative ease and confidence, by the second half of the 1820s many royal names could be read and placed historically through attempts to link them with the Greek-rendered names in Manetho, or by direct inference from their occurrence on standing and museum monuments. A further aid was the Rameses II king list from Abydos (fig. 117), found in 1819, with the result that by 1828 Gardner Wilkinson (1797–1875)[2] was able to produce a fairly comprehensive hieroglyphic list of Egyptian kings from the New Kingdom onward.[3]

However, the canonical excision of the Amarna kings from the Abydos list made their placement problematic. Thus, although Jean-François Champollion (1790–1832) was by 1824 aware of Akhenaten's names, he placed him among a number of other monarchs[4] who, he felt, "appear to have belonged to the XXth dynasty, either on account of similarity to the work of the XIXth monuments, that of the sculptures dating back to the XIXth, *or also because the proper names offer no resemblance to those that Manetho gives to the princes of all other later dynasties, since and including the XXIst.*"[5] Champollion makes, however, no further remarks about the king, but was, nevertheless, of course aware of

FIGURE 117 The king list from the temple at Abydos, showing the adjacent prenomen cartouches of Amenhotep III and Horemheb, with the intervening rulers omitted (BM EA117).

Manetho's late Eighteenth Dynasty list. He thus wondered if "his daughter Acenchêrês" might represent a personal reign by Mutnedjmet (whose name he read as "Tmauhmot"), whom he had noted seated alongside Horemheb (Manetho's "Ôrus") on his so-called coronation statue in Turin during his stay there during 1824–26.[6]

While Champollion was in Turin, the tomb chapels of Tell el-Amarna were visited for the first time by Wilkinson, who was immediately struck by the oddity of their artistic style. He recognized that this style was also to be found on Boundary Stela A, which had been known since 1714, when it was drawn by Claude Sicard (1677–1726), although the latter's published rendering bore little resemblance to the actual piece.[7] Claude Savary (1750–88) had also seen the stela in 1777.[8] The first extensive copies were made in the Amarna tomb chapels by the expedition led by Robert Hay (1799–1863) during 1830–33.

Wilkinson comments that on such monuments "the sun itself is represented with rays terminating in hands . . . which is never seen in other parts of Egypt; In addition to this the name of the King . . . has been purposely effaced, tho I have managed to get a copy of it."[9] He also wondered if these strange monuments might have Persian affiliations—the Persian Period being the principal known era of foreign domination at the time, and thus a possible source of the artistic oddities, especially as true Persian art was as yet little known. He was, however, sure that the mysterious ruler at Amarna was "posterior, at all events, to Thothmes IV."[10] Based on Wilkinson's drawings, Sir William Gell (1777–1836) wondered whether the principal figures (who proved to be Akhenaten and Nefertiti) might be a pair of pregnant women.[11]

Although as yet in the dark concerning Akhenaten, Wilkinson had already identified Tutankhamun's cartouches on an isolated block at Karnak that also bore the name of Amenhotep III. Recognizing that they were thus probably close together in time, he suggested that Tutankhamun might be Amenhotep's brother.[12] Wilkinson also wondered whether the mystery king of Amarna might actually be Tutankhamun, using an alternate name.

Another attempt at naming and placing the Amarna protagonists was made by Nestor L'Hôte (1804–42), in a letter written at Qena on 23 February 1838.

As for the royal personages who address their offerings to the divinity, we see them almost always accompanied by five cartouches, of which two, and the largest, seem to contain, as M. Rosellini thinks, the name and the attributes of the Sun, which was specially revered in Psinaula [a place named in a Roman itinerary with which Amarna was at this time misidentified]. We see them, in fact, placed near the legend of the Sun; but what could give clues to the true intention of these first two cartouches is that they are equally, and almost always, united to the truly royal cartouches. These, three in number, belong to the king, and the third to the queen, who always comes after him. It is to be noted that the word *Atnra* forms the principal element of the names contained in these cartouches, and that thus the legend of the god and that of the prince offer this continual repetition of a name common to the divinity, to the king, and even to the queen, because it is also called *Atara*, plus the qualification of *four times good lady, Nofraït*, with the title of royal wife. As for the proper name of the king, it is completed by three signs which can be pronounced *Bechn* or *Bakhn*. One would be tempted to see there the *Bœon* of chronographers, or even better the *Apachnas*, if one could stick to simple analogies. The cartouche name of which one has the Coptic transcription does not solve the difficulty relative to the place which it must occupy in the list of the ancient kings of Egypt, and the defect of monuments whose criticism can make a useful comparison, allows at most conjectures about it.[13]

This may be the first mention in print of Nefertiti ("Nofraït," "four times good lady" being L'Hôte's understanding of "Neferneferuaten"), the reading of Akhenaten's name as "Bechn/Bakhn-Atnra" corresponding to the state of the art in reading hieroglyphs at that time. "Bœon" and "Apachnas" were the "Bnon" and "[A]pachnan" listed by Manetho as members of the Hyksos Fifteenth Dynasty. This conclusion was not inconsistent with the "otherness" perceived in the art seen at Amarna, but contradicted Wilkinson's view that Akhenaten must have been post–Thutmose IV in date. John Perring (1813–69), who visited Amarna in February 1840, took a similar line to L'Hôte as to the likely date of the material.

It is quite certain that the temples of this race have been destroyed and their names obliterated by the kings of the eighteenth dynasty. . . . From these facts I think it fair to conclude, that these are some of the remains of the shepherd kings, who held Egypt in the period immediately preceding the eighteenth dynasty.[14]

He likewise opined that the cartouches he had seen at Amarna "somewhat resemble[d]" the names given by Manetho for the first three kings of the Fifteenth Dynasty.

Perring nevertheless spotted the link between the Amarna material and the tomb of Ay (WV23), found by Giovanni Battista Belzoni (1778–1823) in 1816, suggesting that as regards the latter king (whose name was at that time being read as "Skhai"),

the features, the protuberant abdomen, the defacement of his name and features in his tomb, and the destruction of his edifices by the kings of the 18th dynasty, appear to identify him with the same intrusive race; and from the similarity of his phonetic name with the first shepherd monarch, I have ventured to place him, but without other authority.

Perring's studies also embraced a number of Amarna blocks that had recently come to light during a partial dismantling of Pylon X at Karnak by the local authorities for building material.[15] Some of them were copied and published by Émile Prisse d'Avennes (1807–79) (fig. 118; also found at this time were the blocks shown in fig. 7).[16]

Although himself clear that the Amarna material could not be pre–Eighteenth Dynasty, and having spotted its likely placement in the latter part of that dynasty, even Wilkinson remained not averse to the idea that there might be some kind of foreign link; writing in 1841, he stated:

The name Atin-re cannot fail to call to mind Attin, or Atys, the Phrygian Sun; and from the ovals of the King, who was noted for the peculiar worship of the Sun represented at the grottoes of Tel el Amarna, being always so systematically erased, some may argue the animosity of the people against a King, who had made an unwelcome foreign innovation in the religion of the country, or at least in the mode of worshipping that Deity. But the name of Atin-re already existed at a very early period; and though the subjects of Tel el Amarna rarely occur, except in those grottoes and the vicinity, some traces may elsewhere be found of the Sun represented with similar rays, in sculptures of the time of the great Remeses.[17]

FIGURE 118 Blocks recovered during the partial demolition of Pylon X at Karnak during 1839–40, giving the names of Amenhotep IV and Nefertiti in their earliest forms.

The 1846 view of Samuel Sharpe (1799–1881) of a typical Amarna wall scene agreed, however, with Wilkinson's earlier thoughts on the date and influences of the material.

> The Persian sun-worship was at this time not unknown in Egypt. On a wall in the city of Alabastron we see carved what we must understand to be Thannyras the [Persian] governor worshipping the sun . . . itself, which is there called Adon-Ra, from the Hebrew title Adonai . . . . The worshipper is called Thaomra the successor of the Egyptian king Adonra-Bakan, a name which seems meant for Thannyras the son of Inarus.[18] The bad state of the sculpture agrees with the fallen state of the nation.[19]

However, Wilkinson's updated position on a much earlier dating for the material had now been reinforced by the discovery of blocks in "Amarna" style alongside others naming a hitherto unknown King Amenhotep (i.e., Amenhotep IV) in Pylon X at Karnak, with Amenhotep's nomen surcharged with the name now being read as "Bekhenaten" in at least one case.

The gender of "Bekhenaten" had continued to be an ongoing matter for debate, both on the basis of the mode of representation seen at Amarna, and on Manetho's attribution of a female ruler to the late Eighteenth Dynasty. In 1845, Baron von Bunsen (1791–1860), in his great multivolume work on Egyptian history and chronology, presented "her" as the wife of Amenhotep IV (by now firmly identified as a son of Amenhotep III), by some confusion also stating that "she" also bore the name "Nefru" (that is, Nefertiti).[20] Richard Lepsius (1810–84) also initially accepted a feminine gender for "Bekhenaten," whom he made the widow and successor of Amenhotep IV.[21] Rather later, Auguste Mariette (1821–81) took a distinctly novel approach in explaining Akhenaten's effeminate appearance, suggesting that he had been captured while campaigning in Nubia and been castrated.[22]

However, following his visits to Amarna and Thebes while leading the great Prussian expedition of 1843–45,[23] which greatly added to the published documentation of the Amarna era, Lepsius finally came to agree with Wilkinson that "Bekhenaten" was not only male, but also the same person as Amenhotep IV.[24] Edward Hincks (1792–1866), writing in 1844, took the same view, but considered (as had Wilkinson) that Tutankhamun was Amenhotep III's brother, that "Skhai" (Ay) was Amenhotep III's son, and that it was he who was father of Amenhotep IV. In Hincks's view, "Skhai" and Amenhotep IV/"Bekhenaten" both ruled in Upper Egypt while Horemheb ("Horus") reigned in the north.[25] This was clearly part of a continuing attempt to reconcile the Amarna kings' omission from the Abydos king list with their now-revealed materiality.

In 1851, Lepsius set out his revised basic configuration of the period,[26] including recognizing the existence of Smenkhkare. This scheme was then incorporated in the next volume of Bunsen's magnum opus (issued in 1856),[27] and the relevant parts of the revised English translation of the whole work. Nevertheless, the emerging relationships of the kings of the period still required correction. Akhenaten, Tutankhamun, and Horemheb were all regarded as sons of Amenhotep III, with Horemheb continuing to face the other two (and Smenkhkare) as rival rulers. Tey, wife of Ay, was also regarded as a further ruling child of Amenhotep III, and as the mother of Rameses I.[28] On the other hand, Nefertiti's place as Akhenaten's wife was secure, albeit under a compressed form of her name, "Nefru," although in 1851 Samuel Birch (1813–85) was attempting to embrace all the hieroglyphs in her cartouche, calling her "Aten-neferu Taiia-nefer."[29]

However, the idea of a foreign influence behind the strangeness of Amarna art and religion endured, even though now divorced from the Hyksos and Persians, Wilkinson's

1854 take on the matter being as follows:

> Towards the latter end of the (18th) dynasty, some "Stranger kings" obtained the
> sceptre, probably by right of marriage with the royal family of Egypt; (a plea on
> which the Ethiopian princes and others obtained the crown at different times,)
> and Egypt again groaned under a hateful tyranny. They even introduced very
> heretical changes in religion, they expelled the favourite god Amun from the
> Pantheon, and introduced a Sun worship unknown in Egypt. Their rule was not
> very long; and having been expelled, their monuments, as well as every record of
> them, were purposefully defaced.[30]

Aside from her mention as, variously, "four times good lady, Nofraït," "Nefru," and
"Aten-neferu Taiia-nefer," Nefertiti does not feature to any great degree in these publications. It was not until the late nineteenth century that substantive speculations began
to appear, when Urbain Bouriant (1849–1903) argued, in 1885, that Nefertiti was a
daughter of Amenhotep III and Tiye, linked with a view that Akhenaten had *not* been
their son.[31] This was based on an understanding of Tiye's titles at Amarna, King's Mother
and King's Great Wife, as "King's Mother *of* the King's Great Wife," that is, Nefertiti.
Although supported by Alfred Wiedemann (1856–1936) a few years later,[32] this reconstruction that denied Akhenaten direct royal lineage gained little traction. Gaston
Maspero (1846–1916) was of the opinion that Nefertiti was a daughter of Amenhotep
III by one of his sisters,[33] while Legrain took the view that she was of lesser birth.[34]

Much more popular was the notion that Nefertiti might have been a foreigner—a
possibility which had also been put forward regarding her mother-in-law, Tiye.[35] As far as
Nefertiti was concerned, this came about following the 1896 publication of the "Amarna
Letters," a cache of cuneiform letters from Levantine and Mesopotamian rulers found
at Amarna in 1887 (with some additional items found there later). Some mentioned
Tadukhepa, the Mitannian princess who had married Amenhotep III and Akhenaten.
This fact was combined with the meaning of the name *Nfrt-iy.ti,* "A beautiful woman has
arrived," to propose that they were one and the same. Although, as noted above (pages
17–18), this presents a range of problems (as was early recognized by even Wallis Budge
[1857–1934][36]), the idea, as initially promoted by Eugène Lefébure (1838–1908),[37] soon
became a "fact"[38] and henceforth a staple of the literature. Flinders Petrie (1853–1942)
took the position that "there can be scarcely a doubt but that [Tadukhepa] is the same
person as the evidently foreign queen Nefertiti."[39]

Yet, as was often done at the time, Petrie interpreted Nefertiti's title *irtt-pʿt* as
"Hereditary Princess" (as in carrying a hereditary right to the throne, with which it is now

clear it has no connection: the title merely denotes membership of the ruling class). He was thus forced to argue that Tadukhepa's father must have "married an Egyptian princess who became mother of Tadukhipa Nefertiti," going further to state that "[s]uch a marriage is very probable, the equality of terms between Dushratta and his brother-in-law Amenhotep III., and his asking as a matter of course for a wife for himself."[40]

Petrie had undertaken the first systematic excavations at Amarna during 1891/92, assisted in part by the young Howard Carter (1874–1939).[41] Large amounts of material were recovered (including our figs. 39, 40, 46, 47, 60, 90), but among the most important historically were large quantities of bezels from finger rings, bearing the names of members of the royal family. These included not only the long-known (in particular from the tomb chapel of Meryre ii) prenomen and nomen of Smenkhkare, but what seemed at the time to be an expanded version of the prenomen, adding "mery-Neferkheperure" or "mery-Waenre" to the core "Ankhkheperure" (fig. 119).

These were accordingly assumed to refer to Smenkhkare, the addition of epithets to a "core" prenomen having been common since the time of Thutmose I, although it was already known that in Rameside and later periods a number of kings could share a "core" prenomen, but be distinguished from each other by different epithets.[42] Petrie further assumed the "long" prenomina were an "earlier" type used by Smenkhkare, dropped when he became a sole ruler.[43]

This assumption was crucial in the final stages of the analysis of the royal names in a graffito in Theban Tomb 139, which had been copied by Wilkinson in the 1820s or 1830s but not published until 1893, by Bouriant.[44] The dateline from this mentioned a King Neferneferuaten-mery-[. . .], whom Bouriant regarded as a new king, "without doubt the Cherrès or Acherrès which we have been given by the Greek lists and who

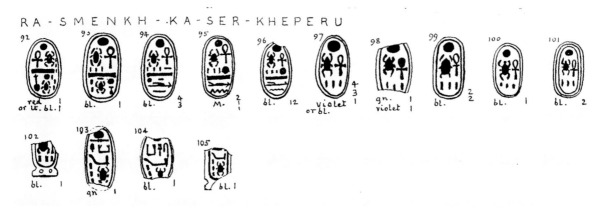

FIGURE 119 Flinders Petrie's drawings of ring bezels from Amarna that he attributed to Smenkhkare, which included the "long" prenomina (92–96) that proved to belong to Neferneferuaten.

have not so far been identified." However, he misread the prenomen in the graffito as "Aakheperure-mery-[. . .]"; as a result he wondered whether the king might be a prince named Aakheperure who had been listed by Lepsius as a son of Thutmose IV.[45] The following year, Vincent Scheil (1858–1940) preferred to read the prenomen as "Neferkheperure-mery-[. . .]."[46] This led Gaston Maspero to conclude that the titulary "seem[ed] . . . to represent a transitional form of the protocol of Amenôthes IV., and not the name of a new Pharaoh."[47] Petrie concurred,[48] as did Henri Gauthier (1877–1950), although the latter noted, most perspicaciously, a further possibility: "a masculinization of the queen, wife of Amenhotep IV, analogous to that known for Hashepsouit."[49]

This remained the position until 1923, when the box lid naming Akhenaten, Neferneferuaten, and Meryetaten together (pages 72–73) was found in the tomb of Tutankhamun. This led to an influential paper by Percy Newberry (1868–1949), published in 1928, which recognized that the problematic sign in the TT139 graffito prenomen was actually "Ankh" and thus represented the same individual named on the newly discovered box—and also on the "long" Ankhkheperure ring bezels from Amarna. Since the latter had already been assessed as belonging to Smenkhkare, Newberry

[i]mmediately recognized that Neferneferuaten "beloved of Uaenrē'" must be the king of the graffito of Tomb No. 139 at Thebes; he was therefore, not a new Pharaoh, but the well-known . . . young king with his consort . . . figured in the tomb of Meryrē' II at El-'Amarnah.[50]

He further expressed no doubts that the "long" and "short" prenomina all belonged to the same person, with "not the slightest doubt that the two forms of the nomen belong to the same Pharaoh." This assessment would not be challenged until the 1970s, and had further implications that will be picked up below (pages 128–29).

Amarna Sunrise

The excavations of Petrie at Amarna greatly advanced the cause of studies into the latter part of the Eighteenth Dynasty, producing a vast amount of new data. This allowed him to end his excavation report with a section on "Historical Results" that disposed of many earlier speculations and presented a basic structure that formed the basis for all future reconstructions. On the other hand, his treatment contained many embellishments that have not stood the test of time, although they have proved very attractive to wider audiences.[51] Two years after his report was issued came the aforementioned first translations of the Amarna Letters (into German,[52] followed almost immediately by an English version).

These new insights into what had hitherto been a problematic and obscure period and place suddenly made Amarna a focus for much wider popular interest. That the Aten cult appeared to be monotheistic added to the attraction, especially when the Great Hymn to the Aten, first published in French translation soon after its discovery in 1884,[53] became available in English during the 1890s.[54] From early on, this work was likened to the Psalms of David, increasing its attraction to the religiously minded. Amarna itself even began to be incorporated into suggested itineraries in major guidebooks, although the extant remains were not impressive for the casual visitor or the uncommitted.[55]

Apart from some work at the Maru-Aten by Alessandro Barsanti (1858–1917) during 1896, substantive fieldwork at Amarna only resumed in 1901, when Norman de Garis Davies (1865–1941) began to comprehensively copy the tomb chapels and boundary stelae on behalf of the UK's Egypt Exploration Fund.[56] This work was just winding down in 1907, when Ludwig Borchardt (1863–1938) arrived to undertake a preliminary survey of the whole of "Greater Amarna," which presaged a large-scale excavation campaign, focused on the southern residential areas of the city between 1911 and 1914. This was undertaken under the auspices of the Deutsche Orient-Gesellschaft, although directly funded by the German textile manufacturer James Simon (1851–1932), who was the formal holder of the concession from the Egyptian authorities.[57]

Shortly before excavations got underway, there appeared a book that would have a long-standing major influence on perceptions regarding the Amarna Period as a whole, and its leading figures in particular. This was a popular biography of Akhenaten by Arthur Weigall (1880–1934), first published in 1910,[58] intended very much for a popular audience and thus containing significant blurring of fact and theory. It presented a highly positive picture of Akhenaten and Nefertiti as people and as proponents of the Aten cult, depicted as a true monotheism. In doing so, it included levels of detail and statements of motivation unrecoverable from the archaeological record, some derived from a likewise-positive presentation by James Breasted (1865–1935) in his 1905-issued *History of Egypt*. Breasted's doctoral thesis had been on the Aten hymns. Both Weigall's and Breasted's books were frequently reprinted and continue to provide parts of the popular audience with their "facts" about the Amarna Period.[59]

The German fieldwork recovered important information regarding domestic architecture, but also made artistic finds, most spectacularly from the sculpture workshop that was associated with a sculptor named Thutmose on the basis of an ivory horse-blinker naming him found in the garden of the attached house.[60] This building lay on the southeastern edge of the Main City (figs. 120, 121) and first began to be revealed at the end of November 1912. Although 141 objects were found spread across the site, the key finds came from two rooms (P.47.2 R18 and R19—fig. 122) where, on 6 and 7 December, some eighty objects were found.[61] These included a large number of portrait heads in plaster (for example, figs. 77, 123), together with semifinished (fig. 58) and unfinished statues (or parts thereof). However, most spectacular were two stand-alone busts, one of Akhenaten and one of Nefertiti, made of limestone, with an outer layer of plaster to allow additional plastic modeling. Such pieces are a kind not generally seen in Egyptian art, and have generally been interpreted as sculptors' models.[62] That of Akhenaten[63] was badly damaged, but that of Nefertiti had suffered only superficial damage (figs. 62, 124).

Although recognized as a spectacular piece from the moment of discovery, the Nefertiti bust was granted to the Berlin share of the season's finds in the division that took place on 20 January 1913, along with the vast majority of the material from the "Thutmose" complex, rather than being retained for the Cairo Museum as a unique piece. The circumstances of the division have been much debated, and a contemporary account indicates that the German team held little hope of retaining the head.[64] However, after an inspection of photographs of all the objects from the season, and a viewing of the objects in their open packing crates, the Inspector of Antiquities for Middle Egypt, Gustave Lefebvre (1879–1957), under whose responsibility Amarna fell, signed a protocol that allocated all pieces made of plaster, plus a range of other objects, to Berlin. These included the painted bust, described rather inaccurately as a "bust in painted plaster of a princess of the royal family." It was placed at the head of the list of Berlin-bound pieces, followed by "a group of twenty-three heads and masks in plaster," and a few other items, including the statuette of Nefertiti from the group (fig. 58).

There are hints that the photographs shown to Lefebvre did not do full justice to the best pieces, and that the inspection of the objects in their crates was not done in the best lighting, although Lefebvre apparently did not request that any be taken out for closer examination. The main crates were then closed and forwarded to the Egyptian Museum in Cairo on 5 February, where those destined for Berlin were given the appropriate export stamp, apparently without further examination. However, the painted bust was diverted to Borchardt's house in Cairo, where it was between 2 and 5 February, after which it seems to have been taken to Berlin as part of the baggage of James Simon's son, Heinrich (1885–1946).[65]

On arrival in Berlin, around 10 February, the bust went to the Tiergartenstraße house of James Simon. As Borchardt was opposed to early public display, the bust was initially shown only to a very small circle of individuals. The rest of the collection arrived in May, including the pieces reserved for Cairo, the Antiquities Service having agreed to their being shown in Berlin before being shipped back to Cairo for permanent display. A small private exhibition of a selection of pieces was put together at Berlin's Neues

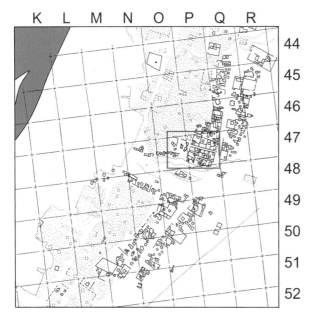

FIGURE 120 The Main City at Amarna, showing the locations of the discoveries of the Berlin painted bust (at O47.20) and Cairo quartzite head of Nefertiti (in house P47.2).

FIGURE 121 Amarna House P47.2, attributed to the sculptor Thutmose.

FIGURE 122 Amarna House P47.2, room 19, the finding place of the painted bust of Nefertiti.

FIGURE 123 Plaster head of Akhenaten from Amarna House P47.2 (Berlin ÄM21351).

FIGURE 124 The Nefertiti bust immediately after discovery, being held by Herbert Ricke and Mohammed el-Senussi, with Paul Hollander behind.

Museum[66] on 15 October, including the Nefertiti bust. The items were then returned to Simon's house on the eighteenth, but were back in the Neues Museum on the twentieth, where Kaiser Wilhelm II viewed them on the twenty-ninth. On 3 November, the monarch was presented with one of two copies of the bust that Simon had commissioned from the sculptress Tina Haim (1887–1974).[67] A later copy made by her in the 1920s has been the basis for all later replicas until the availability of a new mold based on three-dimensional scanning.[68]

A temporary public display then followed at the Museum, which opened to great acclaim, especially from the artistic community,[69] on 5 November 1913. It remained open until June 1914, although with the Cairo-allocated objects replaced by casts in February, when the originals went back to Cairo. Significantly, the exhibition excluded nine pieces, including the undoubted star of the group, the Nefertiti bust, at Borchardt's insistence: doubtless, he was aware of the likely reaction in Egypt—and elsewhere—when it was generally revealed that such a piece had been allowed to permanently leave Egypt.

Amarna Period–mania

The outbreak of war in August 1914 prevented the German team from returning to Amarna that autumn. With the return of peace in 1919, there was no appetite by the British political and French-headed authorities to consider restoring the Germans' permissions, and in 1920 the Amarna concession was given to what had since 1919 been the Egypt Exploration Society (EES, formerly Fund), who would work there almost every season from 1921 to 1936.

Interestingly, it was during the First World War that there appeared what seems to have been the first published work dedicated solely to Nefertiti. Written by a certain M. Worms in the *Journal asiatique*,[70] it notes that the queen had been "greatly neglected by Egyptologists," and gives a comprehensive review of the facts and theories about her down to that date. Worms's own conclusion is that Nefertiti was "a simple

FIGURE 125 Quartzite balustrade from the Maru-Aten at Amarna, with the name and title of Kiya erased and replaced by those of Meryetaten; the king's crown was inlaid in a different material (Ashmolean AN1922.141).

concubine" whom Akhenaten elevated to King's Great Wife around Year 5 from "passion"—corresponding with her appearance on the Early boundary stelae and, in Worms's view, the king's coming of age. After this, articles on the queen, particularly on specific representations of her, became common during the 1920s. A first novel appeared in 1935,[71] and Nefertiti was bracketed with other Egyptian queens in a popular book for young people in 1959[72] before getting her first dedicated book-length treatment, albeit a popular one, in 1964.[73] Others have since followed, although far outnumbered by those that bracket Nefertiti with her husband.

During their very first season, the EES, under the direction of Leonard Woolley (1880–1960), excavated the Maru-Aten, one of the sunshades of the city, and now known to have originally been dedicated for Kiya. Among the finds were a number of reliefs showing the king and a queen adoring the Aten. In all of them the queen's titles and name had been erased and replaced with those of Meryetaten, eldest daughter of Akhenaten and Nefertiti (fig. 125). Although nothing of the original texts was readable, Woolley drew the following conclusions on the basis of Nefertiti being the only then-known wife of Akhenaten.

[H]ere, as nowhere else, the queen's name has in nearly every case been carefully erased and that of her eldest daughter, Meryt-aten, written in palimpsest upon the stone, her distinctive attributes have been re-cut and her head enlarged to the dropsical cranium of the Princess Royal. . . . Nefertiti, if alive, could hardly have agreed to so public an affront, nor would her death have been seized upon by so devoted a husband as an occasion to obliterate her memorials; are we to suppose that things were not so happy as they seemed in the royal household, and that a quarrel so serious as to lose the queen her position put an end to the idyll which had long been the standing theme of court artists?[74]

This idea of a "split" between Akhenaten and Nefertiti soon became a "fact" and was further embroidered in Newberry's aforementioned 1928 study of Smenkhkare. This asserted that the stela of Pay showing the naked Akhenaten and crowned queen Nefertiti (page 71, above) actually depicted[75]

Akhenaten and his coregent Semenekhkarēʿ. The intimate relations between the Pharaoh and the boy as shown by the scene on this stela recall the relationship between the Emperor Hadrian and the youth Antinous.[76]

Warming to his theme, Newberry continued by linking in the apparent evidence from the Maru-Aten:

In regard to this love of Akhenaten for the youth it may be pointed out that . . . at El-Ḥawâtah [Maru-Aten] . . . the queen's name has in nearly every case been carefully erased and that of her eldest daughter, Merytaten, written in palimpsest upon the stone . . . ; are we to suppose that things were not happy as they seemed in the royal household . . .?[77]

The idea that Akhenaten and Smenkhkare were homosexual lovers soon became another staple "fact" of the Amarna Period, and retains wide currency.[78] Indeed, it was not until the "discovery" of Kiya in 1959,[79] and soon afterward the further discovery that she had fallen into disgrace, that the realization dawned that it was *Kiya* who had been replaced by Meryetaten at the Maru-Aten and elsewhere (cf. pages 52, 66–67, above), and thus that the very idea of a "split" between Nefertiti and Akhenaten was pure fiction.[80]

In the meantime, the profile of the Amarna Period had been raised by two particular events. First, in November 1922, the tomb of Tutankhamun had been discovered, its glitter of gold leading to the outbreak of the first epidemic of what was soon dubbed "Tutmania." The young king's intimate links with Akhenaten and Nefertiti brought them yet further into popular focus. Then, in March 1923, the bust of Nefertiti was first revealed to the world.

Simon had placed the collection on permanent loan to the Ägyptisches Museum in 1913, but then presented the whole group to the museum on 11 July 1920. The inclusion of the Nefertiti bust in the resulting permanent exhibition was again opposed by Borchardt, but the museum director, Heinrich Schäfer (1868–1957), a specialist in Egyptian art, nevertheless released photographs to the press in February 1923. He then added the bust to the permanent exhibition in April 1924 and pushed Borchardt to issue the first proper publication of the piece.[81] The reaction to the object was initially surprisingly muted, but its popularity then grew, especially as hints began to emerge that it might be required to return to Egypt.

The Nefertiti Wars

The exhibition of the bust and the appearance of Borchardt's publication shortly afterward finally made the Egyptian authorities aware of its quality. When he became fully aware of the piece, the director of the Egyptian Antiquities Service, Pierre Lacau (1873–1963), rapidly adopted the view that an error must have been made in 1913 and demanded the object's return to Egypt.[82] At the time, Borchardt was engaged in negotiations with Lacau over a resumption of German fieldwork in Egypt. Although he had been received in a far more friendly manner than he had feared, given the events of 1914–18, and had been granted some concessions for surveys and minor excavations, a request to return to Amarna, for which Borchardt had secured funding, was turned down in May 1925. Not only did the EES intend to continue excavations at the site, in spite of a hiatus that had followed the death of their field director, Francis Newton (1878–1924), the previous December, but there was also now a question of rectifying the 1913 "mistake" over the bust. The Egyptian press, in particular *Al-Ahram*, linked this into broader demands for object repatriations and issues surrounding the ongoing clearance of the tomb of Tutankhamun, including allegations that the appearance of the Nefertiti bust had been altered by the Germans to fool Lefebvre.

In October 1929, Lacau met with Schäfer in Berlin. Although the latter demurred at doing a straight swap for a stela that had been the "capital" item of the Cairo portion of the division,[83] they agreed that, in return for rectifying the "mistake" by returning the bust to Egypt, Berlin would receive a pair of important sculptures[84] and a fine Book of the Dead papyrus. However, the deal required the agreement of the Prussian state government, under whose auspices the museum fell. While they were initially supportive, public opinion was outraged at the move.[85] Even a sympathetic letter from Simon, the bust's erstwhile owner, did not help, and huge numbers flocked to Museum Island, where the bust was housed in the Neues Museum building. In the wake of this reaction, the Prussian state withdrew its support for the exchange.

FIGURE 126 The painted bust of Nefertiti on display in Wiesbaden in 1953.

In 1933, following the National Socialist assumption of power in Germany, Hermann Göring (1893–1946), in his role as Minister-President of Prussia, proposed that the bust be returned to Egypt to mark the sixteenth anniversary of the accession of Sultan, and now King, Fuad I of Egypt in 1917. This was part of a wider strategy to gain Egypt as an ally of Germany and, indeed, the return had already been announced to the king at a Cairo diplomatic reception on 10 October 1933, when it was vetoed in March 1934 by the German chancellor Adolf Hitler, who wished to make the bust the focal point of a new Ägyptisches Museum.

The bust of Nefertiti thus remained in Berlin where, along with many other major exhibits, it was crated for potential evacuation following the closure of the Neues Museum on 28 August 1939, shortly before the invasion of Poland that triggered the outbreak of the Second World War. This transfer was soon implemented, and the bust first went to vaults of the Prussian State Bank. Then, in the autumn of 1941, it was shifted to a bunker below Flakturm I, the antiaircraft (Flak) tower adjacent to the Berlin Zoo. Finally, on 6 March 1945, with Soviet forces advancing on Berlin, it was one of a number of pieces moved to a salt mine over 400 meters deep at Merkers-Kaiseroda in Thuringia, which already housed Germany's gold and silver reserves, as well as large numbers of works of art. There, the bust was captured by the US Army and taken first to the Reichsbank in Frankfurt, and then, on 20 August, to the collection depot for recovered art, the Landesmuseum at Wiesbaden, where it was inspected by the US Occupation Zone Military Governor, General Dwight D. Eisenhower (1890–1969), and put on temporary display in February 1946.[86]

During that year, the Egyptian government requested that the US return the bust to Egypt, with the New York Metropolitan Museum of Art suggesting that it first be displayed in New York before going to Egypt. However, the US government took the view in May 1946 that legal ownership remained with Germany—unlike the many war-looted items also now in Wiesbaden—and that the question could only be resolved by a future reconstituted German government. Following the establishment of the Federal Republic of Germany (West Germany) from the Western occupation sectors in 1949, further approaches were made by Egypt in the aftermath of the Egyptian Revolution of 1952, but the German view remained unchanged—that the 1913 division had been legal.

The bust was displayed in Wiesbaden from 1953 to June 1956 (fig. 126), when it returned to Berlin.[87] However, the Neues Museum was now a ruin, hit by British bombs, and lay in the Eastern (Soviet-occupied) sector of the city: the bust went instead to the Western (UK/US/French) sector. Of the prewar collections of the Ägyptisches Museum formerly housed in the Neues Museum, objects that had been hidden in now–West Germany were, during the early 1950s, shifted to storage facilities in West Berlin. The rest of the surviving pieces had, however, been shipped to the Soviet Union in 1945.

Reflecting their celebrity, the only objects for which exhibition space could be found in West Berlin were the Nefertiti bust and some other Amarna pieces. These were accordingly installed in one room of the museum complex at Berlin-Dahlem. However, in 1967 they were moved to one of the former royal bodyguard barracks opposite Charlottenburg Palace (fig. 127) to join the rest of the "Western" Ägyptisches Museum's objects; here they would remain until 2005.

FIGURE 127 The former royal bodyguard barracks at Berlin-Charlottenburg that held the "Western" part of the Berlin Ägyptisches Museum—including the painted bust of Nefertiti—between 1967 and 2005.

FIGURE 128 The derelict hulk of the Neues Museum in Berlin, as it was in August 1990.

In the meantime, the material taken to the Soviet Union had been returned to East Germany in 1958. It was installed in the Bode (formerly Kaiser-Friedrich) Museum building on Museum Island in 1959: the nearby hulk of the Neues Museum remained derelict (fig. 128). It was only with the reunification of Germany in 1989 that work could begin toward reuniting the collections. First, the "Eastern" display was dismantled in 1998, to allow for repairs to the Bode Museum, and some objects moved to Charlottenburg, although most went into temporary storage. Then, in August 2005, Charlottenburg also closed and an interim display of objects from the reunited collection opened in the Altes Museum on Museum Island. This closed in 2008, and many of the objects were sent outside the city in a loan exhibition that ended in Munich in September 2009. The Nefertiti bust, however, remained in Berlin, in a special exhibition at the Kulturforum on Potsdamer Platz.

During the fifteen years prior to this exhibition, work had finally been underway on restoring the Neues Museum building. Reconstruction was carried out in an innovative way that integrated entirely new elements into the surviving original structure, preserving the external aspect without a slavish attempt at replicating the original (fig. 129).[88] This finally reopened on 16 October 2009, with the Nefertiti bust given a position of honor, in a domed chamber all of its own.[89]

The redisplay of the bust led to the latest in the long series of demands for the bust to be returned to Egypt. The Egyptian minister of antiquities, Zahi Hawass, began a campaign in 2002, and in 2007 threatened to suspend German fieldwork in Egypt if the

FIGURE 129 The Neues Museum under repair, and as completed in 2009.

bust was not returned. This followed on from various campaigns during the 1990s, none of which had advanced the position, with Egyptian president Hosni Mubarak undermining the case by being quoted as saying that the bust served as "the best ambassador for Egypt" while in Berlin. The same year also saw the publication of a book that proclaimed the bust a forgery.[90] However, its arguments were rapidly rejected, especially in view of the results of the CT scanning of the piece in 1992 and 2006.[91] Thus, the bust—or "colorful queen," as Borchardt dubbed it at the time of its discovery—remains one of the key icons of the museums of Berlin, as well as ancient Egypt as a whole.

The Pharaoh Who Changed Sex

The identity of Smenkhkare and Neferneferuaten remained a "fact" of the Amarna Period for over four decades following the appearance of Newberry's 1928 article. But then, in 1973, John Harris (1932–2020) noted the presence of a female *t*-sign in some of the "long" Ankhkheperure-prenomina, indicating that the individual bearing that name was thus actually a woman.[92] However, Harris continued to accept that Smenkhkare and Neferneferuaten were the same person, simply changing the sex of that single person. He further argued that this woman was Nefertiti, beginning her reign as Neferneferuaten, with Akhenaten-referencing epithets, and then changing her name to Smenkhkare to mark her status as an independent ruler.

While accepted by some, this proposal was strongly opposed by others.[93] They pointed to, among other things, the depiction in the tomb chapel of Meryre ii and the Memphis block (figs. 74, 75) apparently referring to a Smenkhkare who was married and male. The existence of a male corpse best assessed as that of Smenkhkare (pages 69–70, above) was also noted. A middle way was proposed by Rolf Krauss in 1978, in which he suggested that while Smenkhkare/Neferneferuaten was a man, his wife Meryetaten might have ruled briefly with the feminized prenomen Ankh*et*kheperure.[94]

However, in 1988, James Allen pointed out that the equation of Smenkhkare and Neferneferuaten was not necessarily correct: although their prenomina shared a common core, there was no case where the nomen "Smenkhkare" was found alongside the "long" prenomen, or "Neferneferuaten" alongside the "short" one, which one might have expected if they were actually the same person.[95] Thus, the way was opened toward distinguishing a *male* Smenkhkare and a *female* Neferneferuaten, thereby resolving the issues of both grammar and sexuality: the naked affectional couple on the stela of Pay (fig. 78) were simply husband and wife.[96]

Final proof of Neferneferuaten's gender came in 1998, when Marc Gabolde pointed out that a number of nomen cartouches of Neferneferuaten, whose epithet had formerly been read as "beloved of Akhenaten" (owing to the presence of the $3\underline{h}$-bird), actually contained the epithet $3\underline{h}t$-n-$\underline{h}i.s$—"beneficial for her husband."[97] Nevertheless, while the fact of Neferneferuaten as a female king seems now to have been generally accepted,[98] the question of her pre-kingly identity remained an ongoing matter of debate.

While the fact of this epithet, and also that the female king and Nefertiti shared a name, has persuaded many that Nefertiti and Neferneferuaten were the same person, not all have agreed (cf. page 75, above). One alternate candidate has been Meryetaten,[99] previously mooted as the "mystery female" Ankhetkheperure while Smenkhkare and Neferneferuaten were still held to be a single male individual. Support has been garnered from Manetho's calling his late Eighteenth Dynasty female ruler her predecessor's "daughter"—but this now comes up against the apparently insurmountable problem of her being named alongside Neferneferuaten on the KV62 box fragment.[100]

A further proposal, first put forward by James Allen in 2009,[101] has been that the female king might have been Akhenaten and Nefertiti's fourth daughter, Neferneferuaten-tasherit. This was subsequently withdrawn by its author, who now accepts the equation of Nefertiti and Neferneferuaten.[102] But a version has been revived by Valerie Angenot,[103] who suggests that she ruled alongside her sister Meryetaten, sharing a prenomen, the sisters being the two naked kings depicted on the stela of Pay.[104]

Nevertheless, while these arguments show much ingenuity, Nefertiti still remains the most obvious candidate for being Neferneferuaten with, as just noted, one distinguished supporter of an alternative candidate later changing his position on the matter. On the other hand, in the absence (thus far) of any absolutely unequivocal evidence, the matter of the original identity of Neferneferuaten is likely to remain for some scholars an open question for the foreseeable future.

Looking for Nefertiti

The question of the fate of the mummy of Nefertiti, like that of other "missing" prominent ancient Egyptian figures, has, of course, been present since the potential for its survival had been demonstrated by the discovery of the caches of royal mummies in the late nineteenth century, and of at least semi-intact high-status deposits in the Valley of the Kings. However, it seems not to have been until the end of the twentieth century that the first proposal was made for identifying it with a known body, rather than speculating as to where it might still be buried.

Then, in 1999, Marianne Luban put forward the suggestion that one of the mummies found in the tomb of Amenhotep II (KV35) by Victor Loret (1859–1946) in 1898[105] might be that of Nefertiti.[106] As discovered, KV35 held five groups of human remains: Amenhotep II himself, in his own sarcophagus, but with a new coffin, added during the late Twentieth or early Twenty-first Dynasty; the nine reburied royal mummies in chamber Jb, wrapped and with coffins; the three unwrapped and coffinless mummies in chamber Jc; an unwrapped body in the antechamber; and two skulls in the well shaft.[107] Luban's candidate for Nefertiti was the Younger Lady of the bodies in Jc, although in 2001, Susan James suggested that Nefertiti might rather be the Elder Lady,[108] in spite of this having been identified in 1978 as Tiye on the basis of hair analysis.[109]

These opinions had been on the basis of photographs only, but in 2002/3, Joann Fletcher examined the Younger Lady,[110] apparently the first time someone had done so in some nine decades.[111] On the basis of her observations, including the X-raying of the remains, which were used to produce a facial reconstruction,[112] she proposed that the mummy was indeed that of Nefertiti. However, only a popular book has ever appeared on this work,[113] the lack of any academic publication (and mode of the original announcement via the news media) contributing to a generally negative reaction.[114] The present author argued, like others, that the "Jc three" were in so different a state from the cached bodies in Jb (as discussed above, pages 101–102) that they must have been members of Amenhotep II's family, rather than later reburials.

All this was changed by the DNA testing carried out on a range of mummies either of the Amarna Period, or thought possibly to belong to it.[115] As already noted, the publication of the work proclaimed the Younger Lady to be the mother of Tutankhamun and a sister-wife of Akhenaten, although the raw data subsequently proved capable of other interpretations. We have accordingly argued above that the mummy's genetics could indeed be consistent with the body being that of Nefertiti.

As mothers of kings of Egypt, both the Elder and Younger Ladies were put on display to the press in the Egyptian Museum on 17 February 2010. They were then moved to a permanent location in the vestibule of Room 52, one of the two rooms displaying royal mummies.[116] The Younger Lady was simply labeled as being the mother of Tutankhamun, with no further comment as to her potential identity.

Although a two-dimensional reconstruction had been made for Fletcher's team, a physical three-dimensional model of a reconstruction of the Younger Lady's head was commissioned in 2017 by the *Expedition Unknown* television series (Travel Channel).[117] Fresh scans were undertaken in Cairo in October 2017, from which a 3D-printed replica of the mummy's head was made. This was given to the forensic sculptor Elisabeth Daynès, who had previously produced a reconstruction of the head of the mummy of Tutankhamun and also of a wide range of ancient skulls. She completed work at the end of January 2018 (fig. 109, right).[118]

The value of such reconstructions of skeletonized or mummified heads has been much debated. While there are accepted standards for such work, the thickness of flesh over bone can vary significantly within the accepted limits, while nose and lips are subject to an even greater degree of subjectivity. Thus, any resulting model can rarely be a "true" portrait, only giving one possibility for the subject's appearance in life. As a result, the making of this (or the 2003) reconstruction could never be anything approaching an attempt to "prove" the identity of the mummy. The best that can be said is that the proportions of the face in this case were not inconsistent with the range of the facial type attributed to Nefertiti by ancient artists, in both two and three dimensions.

In contrast to these efforts to demonstrate that the long-known Younger Lady might be the mummy of Nefertiti, in 2015 there appeared a proposal (page 100, above) that implicitly denied such a possibility. In this, Nicholas Reeves argued instead that it lay, presumably untouched, behind a partition wall in the tomb of Tutankhamun. To take this forward, Mamdouh El Damaty, minister of antiquities, approved the use of ground-penetrating radar (GPR), initial work being carried out by Hirokatsu Watanabe, who claimed to have detected chambers behind the north and west walls, containing both metallic and organic material.

This was met by skepticism from GPR specialists, who questioned whether the latter determinations were even possible, while Watanabe was unwilling to share his raw data with others, arguing that his equipment had been so tuned that others would not be able to interpret it. Accordingly, a second set of GPR scans were begun in March 2016, under the auspices of the US National Geographic Society, which did not confirm Watanabe's results.

Accordingly, that May, the new minister of antiquities, Khaled El Enany, commissioned a third GPR survey, carried out over a week during February 2018 by three independent teams, each using a different GPR frequency to provide both depth and definition. Having processed their results separately, their results were compared, with the conclusion that "there is no evidence of doors or empty spaces beyond the funeral chamber up to four meters."[119] In addition, there was no evidence that the potential outlines of a doorway in the north wall that had first sparked Reeves's interest concealed the jambs or lintel of an actual opening.[120]

Nevertheless, further remote-sensing work was carried out during 2019, which did not support the existence of additional rooms in KV62, but did reveal echoes consistent with a descending passage directly north of, and parallel to, that of KV62.[121] If this is indeed a tomb, it will clearly have been sealed by the same flood event as KV55, KV62, and KV63, and based on its location, is almost certainly of the same date of construction. As such, it could be the putative tomb of the princesses originally buried at Amarna (and/or perhaps Nefertiti) posited above (page 99).

The Afterlife of Nefertiti

From the foregoing, it is clear that Nefertiti's modern afterlife has been diverse and wide-ranging. Although she has been apparently consigned to eternal obscurity by her own enemies and those of her family, the past century has seen her become one of the most ubiquitous of all female icons. Much of this has, however, been a result of the painted bust, leading to her general characterization merely as a "famous beauty." Popular hyperbole has also claimed that her looks had been "remembered down the ages"—which is utterly at odds with the reality of Nefertiti's erasure from history and incremental rediscovery in modern times.

Her career has often been presented simply in the shadow of her husband, as the mother of his daughters and even as a bit player in the homoerotic soap opera built around the alleged relationship between Akhenaten and Smenkhkare. It has only been with the realization that the latter was a figment of the imagination and that Nefertiti herself had—to the satisfaction of most, but not all—become a king at the end of her husband's reign that the level of discourse has begun to be raised. Against this background, her key role in the first moves from the "heresy" toward normalization has become clear, while the potential identification of her mummy has raised the specter of a terrible death, presumably at the hands or instigation of her enemies—whether from the forces of revolution or of reaction.

Nevertheless, for most, it is her image, in particular the Berlin bust, that still remains Nefertiti's defining characteristic, an image whose origin may be wholly unknown to the wearer of the earrings, pendant, or T-shirt featuring it. On the other hand, during the Egyptian uprising of 2011, an image by the Egyptian graffiti artist El-Zeft of the Nefertiti bust wearing a gas mask, on a wall on Mohammed Mahmoud Street just off Tahrir Square, became a major icon of the events (fig. 130, left). Closer to her former home, those approaching the modern city of Minya from the Eastern Desert Road are greeted by a colossal rendering of the bust (fig. 130, right), the two cases together underlining the image's role in modern Egypt. Yet Nefertiti's ubiquitous internationality remains one of her defining characteristics—no mean achievement for a woman who died nearly 3,400 years ago and whose enemies had attempted to obliterate her from history.

FIGURE 130 Nefertiti the modern icon. Left: graffito by El-Zeft that existed just off Tahrir Square in Cairo between 2011 and 2014; right: colossal head at the Minya junction of the Eastern Desert Road.

Chronology

LE = Lower Egypt only; UE = Upper Egypt only.
All New Kingdom and Third Intermediate Period dates are based on the scheme set out in Dodson 2019b; in any case, all are more or less conjectural prior to 690 BC. Parentheses indicate a coruler.

EARLY DYNASTIC PERIOD

Dynasty 1	3050–2810 BC
Dynasty 2	2810–2660

OLD KINGDOM

Dynasty 3	2660–2600
Dynasty 4	2600–2470
Dynasty 5	2470–2360
Dynasty 6	2360–2195

FIRST INTERMEDIATE PERIOD

Dynasties 7/8	2195–2160
Dynasties 9/10 (LE)	2160–2040
Dynasty 11a (UE)	2160–2065

MIDDLE KINGDOM

Dynasty 11b	2065–1994
Dynasty 12	1994–1780
Dynasty 13	1780–1650

SECOND INTERMEDIATE PERIOD

Dynasty 14 (LE)	1700–1650
Dynasty 15 (LE)	1650–1535
Dynasty 16 (UE)	1650–1590
Dynasty 17 (UE)	1585–1540
Ahmose the Elder	
Taa	
Kamose	–1540

NEW KINGDOM

Dynasty 18	
Ahmose I	1540–1516
Amenhotep I	1516–1496
Thutmose I	1496–1481
Thutmose II	1481–1468
Thutmose III	1468–1415
(Hatshepsut	1462–1447)
Amenhotep II	1415–1386
Thutmose IV	1386–1377
Amenhotep III	1377–1337
Akhenaten	1337–1321
(Smenkhkare	1325–1323)
(Neferneferuaten	1322–1319)
Tutankhamun	1321–1312
Ay	1312–1308
Horemheb	1308–1278
Dynasty 19	
Rameses I	1278–1276
Sethy I	1276–1265
Rameses II	1265–1200
Merenptah	1200–1190
Sethy II	1190–1185
(Amenmeses [UE]	1189–1186)
Siptah	1186–1178
Tawosret	1178–1176
Dynasty 20	1176–1078

THIRD INTERMEDIATE PERIOD

Dynasty 21	1078–941
Dynasty 22	943–736
Dynasty 23	736–666
Dynasty 24	734–721
Dynasty 25	754–656

SAITE PERIOD

Dynasty 26	664–525

LATE PERIOD

Dynasty 27	525–404
Dynasty 28	404–399
Dynasty 29	399–380
Dynasty 30	380–342
Dynasty 31	342–332

HELLENISTIC PERIOD

Dynasty of Macedonia	332–310
Dynasty of Ptolemy	310–30

ROMAN PERIOD   30 BC–AD 395

NOTES

Notes to Chapter 1

1   Cf. Pamminger 1993; Bickel 2002.

2   Porter and Moss 1952: 168–72; Schiff Giorgini 1965, 1998–2003.

3   Porter and Moss 1952: 166–67; Rilly 2018.

4   Cf. Johnson 1998: 80–94 ("fourth style").

5   Dodson 1990; Maystre 1992: 270–72[62–66]; Wildung 1998.

6   Cf. Robins 1987.

7   Cf. Strudwick 1985.

8   Only two royal sons are known during the Twelfth Dynasty (cf. Dodson and Hilton 2004: 93–94, 96).

9   Thutmose I's eldest son, Amenmose, appears with a high military title (Porter and Moss 1974–81: 46; C.M. Zivie 1976: 52–55; Dodson 1990: 92[5]), followed by Thutmose III's heir, Amenemhat B, who received the office of Overseer of Cattle in his father's Year 24 (Gardiner 1952: 15, pl. ii[57]; Dodson 1990: 92[7]). A King's Son Amenhotep (B) became *sem*-priest of Ptah under Amenhotep II (Pasquali 2007), and under Thutmose IV a King's Son Ahmose (B) functioned as high priest at Heliopolis (Porter and Moss 1934: 59; Moursi 1972: 52–56).

10   Named daughters Iset C, Henuttaneb A, and S[it]amun are shown at Soleb (Porter and Moss 1952: 170[7]; Schiff Giorgini 1998–2003: V, pl. 97), with generic female children at Soleb (Schiff Giorgini 1998–2003: V, pl. 94, 127, 131), and in TT192 (Epigraphic Survey 1980: pl. 47, 57).

11   E.g., JE33906, from Medinet Habu (Porter and Moss 1960–64: 774).

12   Hayes 1951: fig. 27[KK].

13   In the mortuary temple of the pyramid at Meidum (Petrie 1894: pl. xxxvi[XVIII]: cf. Dodson 2009).

14   Classic statements in favor include (e.g.) Aldred 1959; 1968: 100–16; 1988: 169–82; and Giles 2001: 25–137, with a rather different approach taken in Johnson 1996; the contrary case has been put in, for example, Redford 1967: 88–169; Murnane 1977: 123–69, 231–33; Gabolde 1998: 62–98; Dorman 2009.

15   Jar labels from Malqata (Hayes 1951: 87; Aldred 1988: pl. 68).

16   To judge from the point at which regnal year number changes within a set of texts from Years 5/6 (Murnane 1976).

17   Although anything significantly beyond an incomplete Year 39 would imply that he was no longer resident at Malqata during a hypothetical Year 40 or beyond, given that every year between 28 and 38 is attested in Malqata documents, as is Year 1 of (presumably) Amenhotep IV (see Hayes 1951: fig. 16).

18   Cottevieille-Giraudet 1936; Porter and Moss 1972: 20, 24, 37, 39–40, 53, 182–83, 190–91, 211, 244, 296–97, 339, 460, 540; Smith and Redford 1976; Lauffray 1980; Redford 1984: 63–71; 1988; Vergnieux 1999. It should be noted that a number of military scenes originally attributed to Amenhotep IV's buildings (see A. Schulman in Redford 1988: 53–79) have now been identified as deriving from a temple of Tutankhamun (Johnson 2009).

19   Van Dijk 2008.

20   For the names of Aten, see Gunn 1923.

21   Another block from the same "classical" group was recorded at the end of the 1830s, but is now lost (Prisse d'Avennes 1847: pl. xi[center-left]), while others remain in situ (Redford 1984: 64, figs. 4.4–5).

22   This was essentially an elaboration of the old hieroglyph for "sunshine."

23   Nefertiti's name appears on the block shown in part in our fig. 7b, but as it is in the Neferneferuaten-Nefertiti form apparently adopted around Year 4/5 (p. 26), it is presumably secondary: certainly, the king's nomen was updated from its Amenhotep to its Akhenaten form.

24   Cf. Nims 1973; Ertman 2009.

25   Cf. Werner 1979 for the similarities in the iconographies of the king and queen.

26   Redford 1984: 71.

27   Porter and Moss 1972: 208–15.

28   On the other hand, it has also been suggested (Carlotti and Martinez 2013) that the ḥwt-bnbn material came from a colonnaded courtyard in front of Pylon III, occupying much of the area later covered by the Great Hypostyle Hall of Sethy I.

29   Loeben 1994a.

30   Morkot 1986; Ertman 2006; Matić 2017.

31   Samson 1977.

32   Blankenberg-van Delden 1969: 16, 21–56, 149–53; a number of further examples have been published subsequently, which is also the case for other series of scarabs mentioned later. For Amenhotep III's "commemorative" scarabs in general, cf. Baines 2003.

33   AL 23; for translations of all Amarna Letters, see Moran 1992.

34   AL 26.

35   AL 27.

36   AL 28, 29.

37   Edel 1997.

38   Ranke 1935: 201[12].

39   Ranke 1935: 10[7–8].

40   On a debate on the correct reading of the name initiated by Sethe 1905: 135, see N. de G. Davies 1903–1908: 18 n.1; Aldred 1968: 105–106; Hari 1976; Dodson 2018a: 98–99.

41   TA6 (Panehsy—N. de G. Davies 1903–1908: II, pl. v, viii), TA7 (Parennefer—N. de G. Davies 1903–1908: VI, 4, pl. iv), TA8 (Tutu: N. de G. Davies 1903–1908: VI, 10, pl. xvi), TA14 (May—N. de G. Davies 1903–1908: V, pl. iii, v), TA20 (anonymous—N. de G. Davies 1903–1908: V, pl. xv), and TA25 (Ay himself—N. de G. Davies 1903–1908: VI, pl. xxvi).

42   Habachi 1958.

43   Dodson 2018a: 99.

44   Cairo JE35626, apparently from Sheikh Abd el-Qurna (Helck 1955–58: 1908–10).

45   Hawass et al. 2010.

46   Lorenzen and Willerslev 2010; Marchant 2011; 2013: 196–211.

47 For a conspectus of theories down to 2001, see Grimm 2001.

48 Gabolde 2013; 2015: 93–97.

49 Ockinga 1997.

Notes to Chapter 2

1 Perhaps since the beginning of the Third Dynasty, certainly since the middle of the Fourth Dynasty.

2 Troy 1986: 160; it is unclear whether the attribution of the title to Mertseger, apparently wife of Senwosret III, in a text of Thutmose III in the temple at Semna-West, accurately reflects her actual title, or simply Eighteenth Dynasty convention.

3 Reeves 1978; it otherwise only seems to appear in the tomb chapel of Ay and a few architectural fragments.

4 Aat, a wife of Amenemhat III of the Twelfth Dynasty, had been, uniquely, ḥnwt-t3w.

5 Earlier, it had been used by Hetepti, the mother of Amenemhat IV, who seems not to have been the son of a king.

6 See, conveniently, Troy 1986: 167[18.41].

7 Nims 1973: 186, n.63; Smith and Redford 1976: 80.

8 Murnane and van Siclen 1993: 51[n].

9 Plaster from house N49.19.2 (exc. no. 21/449, now in the Rosicrucian Museum, San Jose; hand copy at www.flickr.com/photos/egyptexplorationsociety/18674374110/in/album-72157654641493541/).

10 Rammant Peeters 1985; on Amarna Period royal headgear in general, see Green 2000.

11 Smith and Redford 1976: 81.

12 On the issue, see Ertman 1976.

13 Ertman 1992.

14 See Gohary 1992; Redford 1994.

15 E.g., Traunecker 1986.

16 Gohary 1992: 30–33.

17 Redford 1984: figs. 10–11.

18 Johnson 2012–13. The fact that the statues had been recut was first noted by Kozloff (2010, 2012), but assuming that the original owner was Amenhotep III.

19 See Manniche 2010 for a full documentation and discussion of the sandstone figures.

20 Cf. Aldred 1968: 133–39; 1988: 231–36; Vishnoi 2000.

21 Manniche 2010: 93–96.

22 Johnson 2017.

23 Cf. Smith and Redford 1976: 83.

24 Smith and Redford 1976: pl. 32[5], 33[5].

25 Aldred, who was a leading proponent of a long coregency between Amenhotep III and IV, on the other hand suggested that the younger king was sterile and that Amenhotep III was the father of Nefertiti's children, the label distinguishing them from those borne to him by Tiye (1968: 137–38).

26 Murnane and van Siclen 1993.

27 R.A. Wells 1987; 1989.

28 For the latest edition of this text, see Murnane and van Siclen 1993: 11–68; see also Murnane 1995: 73–81.

29 Williamson 2016: 16–18, 174–75.

30 Williamson 2016: 18–25; it has been suggested that one may have existed for Neferneferuaten-tasherit at Amarna, and even one for Ankhesenpaaten at Memphis (Pasquali 2011). A large quartzite slab, reused at Heliopolis (our fig. 65), seems to have come from a sunshade of Meryetaten, perhaps also at Memphis (Wegner 2017).

31 Williamson 2016: 9–14.

32 Williamson 2016.

33 Williamson 2016: 26–165.

34 Williamson 2016: 172–81.

35 Williamson 2016: 162–65.

36 It has been suggested that Kom el-Nana as a whole may have been a

center for mortuary cults (Williamson 2017), although this may be an overinterpretation of the presence of sunshades within royal memorial temples of the earlier and later New Kingdom.

37   Martin 1974, 1989; Dodson 2018–19.

38   Not, as early interpreters took it, that Akhenaten himself would never leave the city—contradicted by the provision for the return of his and the royal family's bodies for burial if they died elsewhere; cf. Murnane and van Siclen 1993: 169–71.

39   Porter and Moss 1934: 230–32; Murnane and van Siclen 1993; Fenwick 2006.

40   Ikram 1989.

41   On the basis that she only appears in certain scenes, and on a much smaller scale than her three elder sisters.

42   For a summary of the appearance of the princesses in the various Amarna tomb chapels, see N. de G. Davies 1903–1908: II, 6–7.

43   Weatherhead 2007: 91–106.

44   Roeder 1969: pl. 106[831-VIIIA].

45   Roeder 1969.

46   Roeder 1969: pl. 105[56-VIIIA].

47   Although Roeder (1969: pl. 105[56-VIIIA]) suggests an alternative restoration comprising Akhenaten's prenomen, followed by "[beloved of] Aten"; however, there are few parallels, and the princess's name seems the more likely restoration.

48   See Dodson 1990.

49   Huber (2016: 114) makes no mention of this, and also misses the crucial point of substantive office versus mere birth when citing a representation of Crown Prince Thutmose in the company of Amenhotep III (Munich Gl93; see conveniently Dodson 2014a: fig. 33) as "disproof" of the nonrepresentation of princes prior to the reign of Akhenaten: Thutmose's

presence is in his role as high priest of Ptah, not surprisingly, as the context is the burial of an Apis bull, the "Herald of Ptah." Huber also cites a scene on the back of Pylon III at Karnak as an example of Prince Amenhotep shown with his father—but this is actually an image of Tutankhamun, secondarily inserted into the scene (see Dodson 2018a: 70–71, with fig. 54).

50   However, others have argued for other fathers for Tutankhuaten: proponents of the theory of a long coregency between Amenhotep III and Akhenaten have often made him a younger brother of the latter (e.g., Desroches-Noblecourt 1963: 133–36; Aldred 1968: 96–99), while others have proposed that his father was Smenkhkare, by an otherwise unknown sister (Allen 2016: 10–11) or by Akhenaten's eldest daughter Meryetaten (e.g., Huber 2016; 2019a; 2019b). Huber (2019b: 21) attempts to undermine the implication of the Ashmunein pair of blocks that Tutankhamun and Ankhesenpaaten shared a father by adopting Roeder's restoration (n.47, above), and suggesting that it indicates different fathers for the two children.

51   A convenient summary of facts and theories about Kiya is to be found in Kramer 2003; see also Quiring 1960, Manniche 1975, Reeves 1988, and van Dijk 1997. Redford (1984: 150) suggested that Tadukhepa's aunt, Gilukhepa, might have become Kiya; cf. Helck 1984. Birrell 1987 puts forward a case for Kiya being a daughter of Ay.

52   Peet and Woolley 1923: 109–24; Badawy 1956; Thomas 1982.

53   In spite of being only shown with female offspring, like Nefertiti, Kiya has often been proposed as the mother of

Tutankhaten, following the rejection of Nefertiti on the grounds of only being shown with daughters!

54   Cf. Gabolde 1992 for a proposal (supported by van Dijk 1997: 37) that Beketaten might be this daughter of Kiya, with her representations with Tiye to be regarded as reflecting a foster relationship after Kiya's disgrace.

55   Petrie 1894: pl. xxv[95].

56   Van Dijk 1997: 36–37.

57   On the potential actual meaning of this formulation, cf. Gunn 1923; Assmann 1984: 245; 1992: 164–65; 1993: 33; Hornung 1999: 76–78.

58   Murnane and van Siclen 1993: 103–104.

59   TA1 and 2, for which see page 60.

60   Cf. Fairman in Pendlebury 1951: 185.

61   Cf. Györy 1998; one of the South Tombs Cemetery coffins bears the Four Sons of Horus—contrasting with Atenist invocations on others (Kemp 2012: 261–62).

62   This echoes similar issues over whether early mentions of "the Aten" refer to a deity or simply the physical globe of the sun.

63   Mut's name is still intact in one scene in TA25 (Ay—N. de G. Davies 1903–1908: VI, pl. xxvi) and two in TA14 (May—N. de G. Davies 1903–1908: V, pl. iii, v), while it has been erased in TA7 (Parennefer—N. de G. Davies 1903–1908: VI, 4, pl. iv); in TA6 (Panehsy—N. de G. Davies 1903–1908: II, pl. v, viii), TA8 (Tutu—N. de G. Davies 1903–1908: VI, 10, pl. xvi) and TA20 (anonymous—N. de G. Davies 1903–1908: V, pl. xv). Mutnedjmet's name and titles have been largely destroyed, leaving the status of the Mut vulture unknown in these cases.

64   T.M. Davis 1910: 14; unfortunately this section of the text is only available in hieroglyphic type, no extant drawing or photograph allowing it to be collated.

65   Although the goddess Maat's name came to be spelled out, avoiding the use of her ideogram.

66   Murnane 1995: 113–16 (tomb chapel of Ay).

67   Montserrat 2000: 36–37.

68   Cf. Freed 1999.

69   See Manniche 2010: 135–43 for a useful overview.

70   See Manniche 2010: 131–33.

71   E.g., Thompson 2004; 2006.

72   Pendlebury 1933: 117–18.

73   A wine jar docket of a Year 1 and a finger ring of Tutankhamun were found in the complex.

74   Porter and Moss 1934: 202–203; see further pages 117–20, 123–28.

75   Phillips 2004; Bodziony 2007; Thompson [2012].

76   Bednarski 2009.

77   Durham 1964/188+1964/213+UPMAA E16022a-b, from Buhen (H.S. Smith 1976: 124–29, pl. xxix, lxxv); Darnell and Manassa (2007: 127) do, however, propose that the durbar was fundamentally a celebration of that Nubian campaign.

78   Kemp et al. 2013; Dabbs, Rose, and Zabecki 2015; Kemp and Rose 2016; Kemp 2017: 137–49; Stevens et al. 2018.

Notes to Chapter 3

1   Raven 1994: 7–8; Brock 1996: 11, 16; Gabolde 1998: 132–34; it should be noted that the fragments attributed to this object in Martin 1974: 28–30 actually came from the sarcophagus of Queen Tiye.

2   Van Dijk 2009.

3   Cf. Panagiotakopulu 2004.

4   For whose burial see Raven 1994; Brock 1996.

5   Hanke 1978: 142–45.

6   Hanke 1978: 150–54; cf. Gabolde 1998: 121–22 n.997.

7   The latter the view of Helck 1984: 21.

8   While there have been examples of births to children aged under ten, they are extremely rare.

9   A further lost block once thought to include a depiction of Smenkhkare walking behind Akhenaten has now been shown to be a product of overenthusiastic modern graphical restoration (Málek 1996).

10   Although some have on occasion tried to interpret these items as giving Meryetaten the prenomen Ankhkheperure, a pairing of the king's prenomen with the name of his wife is by no means unknown.

11   Cairo JE62654 (Beinlich and Saleh 1989: 20[46gg]; Dodson 2020a: fig. 5).

12   Cairo JE62172 (Loeben 1991, 1994a).

13   Dodson 2018a: 27–29.

14   Mallinson 1989: 126.

15   See the corpus of Petrie 1894: pl. xv, extended in Frankfort and Pendlebury 1933: pl. xlix.

16   Shaw 1984; Shannon 1987; Pendlebury 1951: 75, pl. c[22, 23, 24]; Kemp 2008–2009: 45; cf. Dodson 2018a: 144–45 n.29, and page 143 n.42, below, on issues with the reporting of material naming Smenkhkare.

17   Pendlebury 1951: 194.

18   G.E. Smith 1912: 51–56 (25/26±2–3 years of age at death); Harrison 1966 (17–25); Filer 2000; 2002 (20–25); Germer 2001 (18–23/25); Strouhal 2010 (19–22).

19   Hussein and Harris 1988; Harris and Hussein 1991: 238 (~35); Hawass et al. 2010: table 1 (35–45).

20   Cf. Strouhal 2010: 110 on the lack of any justification of the Hawass et al. 2010 estimate (restated "33–35," again without discussion, in Hawass and Saleem 2016: 84–86).

21   There have been many modern proposals for post–Middle Kingdom coregencies that are based on circumstantial evidence only, rather than unequivocal ancient records: see the discussion in Dodson 2014b.

22   Johnson 2018: 75.

23   See below, page 129, for an alternate view.

24   Akhenaten seems to have come to the throne at the beginning of I prt and died before the end of his seventeenth regnal year, the latter thus falling fifteen and a half months after the date in question.

25   van der Perre 2014.

26   The woman in question, Merneith, was buried in the kingly cemetery at Abydos, Umm el-Qaab, in a tomb of the same type as kings of the same period, with a monumental enclosure on the edge of the desert; the principal difference was that the twin stelae marking the offering place did not enclose her name in a kingly serekh (Seipel 1980: 23–45).

27   Callender 1998; the alleged early First Intermediate Period queen regnant "Nitokris," mentioned in the Greek works of Herodotus and Manetho, seems to be a phantom of scribal confusion: see Ryholt 2000.

28   Works on Hatshepsut are numerous, with Roehrig 2005 a good digest.

29   Cairo JE61495 (Beinlich and Saleh 1989: 31–32[79+574]); the actual box was apparently inscribed from the outset for Tutankhamun and Ankhesenamun, although with a fastening knob made in the name of Neferneferuaten, with Tutankhamun's nomen superimposed. Oddly, Edwards 1972: [17], while noting the palimpsest on this knob, states there was "no trace of an erased inscription [under] all the other cartouches on the box," contradicting the observations not only of Beinlich and Saleh, but of Howard

Carter himself on his original record cards (Griffith Institute, Oxford), who provides both hand copies of the palimpsest names and comments that the object was "without doubt originally for Smenkh-ka-Re & his wife Mert-Aten" (on the then-current view that Smenkhkare and Neferneferuaten were the same person).

30   Cairo JE62416–7 (Beinlich and Saleh 1989: 222[620(40–42)]).

31   Roeder 1969: pl. 10[826-VIIIA]; Hanke 1978: 204; Gabolde 1990: 41 fig. 9; 1998: pl. xxiv.

32   Johnson 2018: 73–75.

33   Weatherhead 2007: 257–59[12.1–3]; while one nomen cartouche (12.1) is correctly read, the other pair is misinterpreted as belonging to Akhenaten.

34   Kemp and Stevens 2010: 11–185.

35   Kemp and Stevens 2010: 119–29.

36   Kemp and Stevens 2010: 95–103.

37   Peet and Woolley 1923: 23.

38   Stewart 1976: 22, pl. 12[52.2]; Allen 1988: 117–21, albeit with rather different conclusions; cf. also Gabolde 1990; 1998: 162–66, pl. xxiv; Martin 2009.

39   Pendlebury 1951: 74 (southeast courts), 107 (magazine P41.1/3).

40   Petrie 1894: 29.

41   Frankfort and Pendlebury 1933: 50, 52.

42   Shannon 1987; it should be noted that a full understanding of the number of Neferneferuaten bezels found in excavations is hindered by her material historically being lumped with the items naming Smenkhkare and reported under his name. For example, Pendlebury 1951: 74 lists the discovery of two "Smenkhkarē'" faience rings at Amarna: checking the type codes indicates that while one indeed refers to Smenkhkare (reading "Ankhkheperure"), the other

actually reads "Ankhkheperure-mery-waenre," that is, Neferneferuaten. Verifying the actual reading is not always straightforward, as while this can be found in most later reports via a type code, this is not provided in earlier ones (including Peet and Woolley 1923). In addition, only "new" types are illustrated in the volumes publishing the interwar Egypt Exploration Society work at Amarna, readers being referred to Petrie 1894, but under fresh type codes, which can only be understood by consulting one of the appendices of Frankfort and Pendlebury 1933!

43   The episode is described in fragment 28 of the *Deeds of Shuppiluliuma* (published in Güterbock 1956: 94–98, 107–108), found at Boghazkale (Hattusa) in Anatolia. There is a wide literature on the topic, with Bryce 1990 and Murnane 1990: 22–31 important sources; see also Dodson 2018a: 89–94.

44   In spite of an attempt to bolster the Nefertiti option by identifying a certain "Armaya," mentioned in a fragmentary Hittite text, with Horemheb as deputy of Tutankhamun (Stempel 2007, subsequently followed by others, e.g., Theis 2011). This would result in Shuppiluliuma's death preceding that of Tutankhamun, thus excluding identifying the Egyptian queen as his widow, and accordingly moving the events back to the death of Akhenaten (or Smenkhkare, if one were to reject our preferred reconstruction and give him an independent reign: Meryetaten has also been put forward as a candidate for *dakhamunzu*). However, while "Armaya" might indeed be a Hittite writing of "Horemheb," the latter is a sufficiently common name to make it impossible to rely on the mention of this name alone to confidently push the episode back to

that time. It may be noted that Marc Gabolde (1998: 187–226), in accepting such a dating, also proposed that a Hittite prince actually arrived in Egypt, married Meryetaten, and became Smenkhkare before his demise. Of course, this is impossible on our view that the reign of Smenkhkare was wholly within that of Akhenaten; for one detailed refutation, see Sadowska 2000.

45   Porter and Moss 1960–64: 253[5]; Dodson 2020b.

46   Haring 1997, 25–29.

47   Allen (2016: 10) objects to this on the basis of the fact that Thutmose III's memorial temple is called both "ḥnqt ꜥnḫ Menkheperre" and "ḥnqt ꜥnḫ Menkheperre-meryamun." However, this misses the crucial point that no other king of the period was called Menkheperre, and that until the late Eighteenth Dynasty the use (or nonuse) of epithets was fairly promiscuous and never served to distinguish one king from another, particularly as all had in any case unique core prenomina. It was only when a core was repeated for more than one king that this became an issue and epithets accordingly became fixed as integral parts of the prenomen. This is indisputably the case during the Twentieth Dynasty and onward, when Rameses III and a number of his successors reused the core name "Usermaatre" with the addition of unique distinguishing epithets. This continues and elaborates during the Third Intermediate Period, where in some cases it requires analysis of the epithets within both the prenomen and the nomen to identify the king in question. Neferneferuaten stands at the very beginning of this process, with her clear need to distinguish her prenomen from that of Smenkhkare.

48   Which was certainly the case during the Twelfth Dynasty, and also in the Third Intermediate Period case of Osorkon III and Takelot III.

49   The nearest one could probably get is the case of Catherine II of Russia, who seized the throne from her husband Peter III, with their son Paul not becoming emperor until Catherine's death. However, this was a case of usurpation, rather than planned transition.

50   This would appear to have lain behind the later depiction of the former general Ay carrying out the burial of Tutankhamun on the wall of the latter's burial chamber.

51   There have been a number of suggestions that the throne might have been originally made for another (e.g., Ertman 2003, but see the discussions by Eaton-Krauss 2008a: and 2008b: 31–32).

52   On the date of the stela, cf. J.R. Harris 1973c.

53   El-Khouly and Martin 1987.

54   Hoffmeier and van Dijk 2010; T.W. Davis 2019: 324–25, fig. 7.87.

55   Buvot 2003: 219–21[88], who queries whether the Louvre fragment might have belonged to another royal lady of the period.

56   Loeben 1986; 1999; cf. Allen 2009: 18.

57   S.T. Smith 1992.

58   And actually depicted in two dimensions on the walls of the tomb of Sethy II (KV15), perhaps owing to problems with supplying him with actual examples.

59   Cairo JE60715; the difference between them is, however, recorded as being a matter of "Theban" versus "El Amarna" art in Howard Carter's record cards (289a, 289b) from the tomb.

60   For a comprehensive (if now somewhat outdated in places: cf. chapter five) overview and discussion, see J.R. Harris 1992.

61 E.g., Cairo JE61949, on which the Tutankhamun cartouche is the wrong way around, suggesting that it may have been replaced.

62 Cairo JE61517 (McLeod 1970: 10–12, pl. 17, 20).

63 The cartouches on the front of the middle coffin are sunk slightly more deeply into the wood than the surrounding texts, which may support their having been changed.

64 One option is that although Smenkhkare had commissioned a "traditional" set of funerary equipment, Akhenaten was unwilling to bury his coregent with it, accordingly improvising an "Atenist" outfit from the coffin and canopic jars manufactured for the now-disgraced Kiya (which were found in KV55), and Smenkhkare's coffin and canopic coffinettes put into store until resurrected for, first, Neferneferuaten, and then Tutankhamun.

65 *Pace* the previous assertion by the present writer (Dodson 1994: 213; 2002).

66 Eaton-Krauss 1993: 13–23; Dodson 1996.

67 Engelbach 1940: 138; J.R. Harris 1992: 61, 70 nn.91–95.

68 Suggestions have also been made that the gold mask found on Tutankhamun's mummy had been taken over from Neferneferuaten, including replacing its face and altering the cartouche in one of its inscriptions (Reeves 2016). However, a detailed technical examination has revealed no evidence of either (Broschat, Eckmann, and Seidlmayer 2016).

69 Although Fletcher 2004: 373–77 had suggested that damage had been inflicted maliciously not long after mummification.

70 Hawass and Saleem 2016: 80–83.

71 For which see the summary in Dodson 2019a: 74–79.

Notes to Chapter 4

1 Dodson 2018a: 64–66.

2 Eaton-Krauss and Murnane 1991; Forbes 2000.

3 Petrie Museum UC23806 (Petrie 1894: pl. xv[117]); UC1927 (Samson in Pendlebury 1951: 230, pl. cviii).

4 In the sanctuary of the Great Temple were found various fragments dating to his reign (e.g., Pendlebury 1951: pl. lx[3]; Petrie 1894: 43, pl. xi[5]).

5 Although there has been a wide range of ideas as to the original configuration of the deposit, this seems to be the most straightforward reading of the extant data.

6 This deposit's publication is in preparation by Salima Ikram. There seems far too much material to have come from a single burial. The style of the coffins used to hold much of the material makes it clear that they were made during the reign of Amenhotep III, while the tomb itself was sealed by the flood that covered the sites of KV55 and Tutankhamun's KV62 soon after the latter was sealed, leaving the Amarna Royal Tomb the most likely place of origin of the KV63 material.

7 Stephen Cross, personal communication.

8 Reeves 2015; 2019.

9 As noted in Robins 1984.

10 Wong et al. 2012.

11 A novel variation on the latter idea (in Huber 2018 and Haas Dantes 2018) has been to reinterpret the whole wall, including making the central scene of Tutankhamun before Nut originally a scene of the marriage of Akhenaten and Nefertiti. While ingenious, the arguments deployed are subjective in the extreme and propose original tableaux that have no parallels in Egyptian art or the iconography of the decoration of tombs.

12 Regarding the discontinuities between the north and other walls of the burial chamber, it is perfectly possible that this is an artifact of the construction of the tomb, with the north wall prepared first, perhaps even before the introduction of the sarcophagus. Given that the other walls include the partition wall between the antechamber and the burial chamber, which can only have been decorated after the funeral and the erection of the shrines around the sarcophagus, there may have been some rethinking in the interim of both the proportions to be used and the color scheme, resulting in the final state of the decoration.

13 Cross 2008; 2009; 2014; older ideas based on the belief that the area remained accessible into Rameside times have now to be discarded.

14 As first noted by Arthur Weigall: cf. Aldred 1968: 149–50.

15 Kawai 2013.

16 Although there are potential signs of interference in two cases (Reeves 1990: 198–99).

17 Where one of his toes was found. At least one son of that king, Webensenu, is known from canopic equipment to have been buried with his father; see further chapter five, n.116, below.

18 I fail to understand Reeves's arguments (1990: 198) for the opposite order.

19 Gaballa 1977: 25.

20 Using the redaction of Josephus; for this and other versions, see Waddell 1940: 101–47.

Notes to Chapter 5

1 For histories of Egyptology, see Thompson 2014–19; Bednarski, Dodson, and Ikram forthcoming.

2 Biographical notes on Wilkinson, and many of the other scholars mentioned in this chapter, are available in Bierbrier 2019.

3 J.G. Wilkinson 1828–30.

4 The others being Pepy I, Nakhthorheb, Amenemhat II, Osorkon I, Herihor, and Menkare—a motley selection ranging in actuality from the Sixth to the Thirtieth Dynasties.

5 Champollion 1824–26: 2:106 (author's translation from the French), with pl. v.

6 Champollion 1824–26: 1:56, 85–86.

7 van de Walle 1976: 12–19.

8 van de Walle 1976: 18–19.

9 Letter dated 13 August 1925, quoted in J. Thompson 1992: 68.

10 J.G. Wilkinson 1830: 21.

11 J. Thompson 1992: 67–68.

12 J.G. Wilkinson 1828–30: 118.

13 L'Hôte 1840: 55–56 (author's translation from the French).

14 Perring 1843: 144.

15 Cf. Gliddon 1841: 47–67.

16 Prisse d'Avennes 1843: 76–92; 1847: pl. x, xi.

17 J.G. Wilkinson 1841: 297–98.

18 Inaros (II) was an Egyptian rebel against the Persians around 460 BC.

19 Sharpe 1859: 199.

20 Bunsen 1845–57: 3:88–89.

21 The idea that Akhenaten was a woman endured in some quarters until the end of the 1880s: Lefébure 1891: 478–83.

22 Mariette 1855: 57.

23 For its records from Amarna, which the expedition visited from 19 to 21 September 1843 and 7 to 14 June 1845, see Lepsius 1849–59: pl. 91–111; 1897: 123–49.

24 Lepsius 1853: 262 n.278.

25 Hincks 1848: 105–13.

26 Lepsius 1851.

27   Bunsen 1845–57: 4:162.

28   Bunsen 1854: 539–42. In this equation, she is confounded with Tyti, wife of Rameses III (QV52); Tyti had the additional title of King's Mother, which when thus applied to Tey, is used as the basis for making the latter Rameses I's mother.

29   Birch 1851: 407.

30   J.G. Wilkinson 1854: 1:308.

31   Bouriant 1885: 52; curiously, Nefertiti is not mentioned by name in this paper, just implicitly as the wife who made Akhenaten Tiye's son-in-law.

32   Wiedemann 1895: 156–57.

33   Maspero 1896: 316–17 n.6.

34   Legrain in Bouriant, Legrain, and Jéquier 1903: 34 n.1.

35   For an overview of the discussion, see Maspero 1907: xix–xxi; 1896: 315 n.1; cf. Dodson 2019c: 9–13.

36   Budge 1902: 4:114–15.

37   Lefébure 1891: 478.

38   Cf. Bryant and Read 1893: 206.

39   Petrie 1899: 229.

40   Petrie 1899: 210–11.

41   Petrie 1894.

42   The first example of this was Rameses III, who shared the core Usermaatre with Rameses II, but used the epithet "meryamun" rather than the earlier king's "setepenre." This approach then became common, Rameses IV being initially "Usermaatre-setepenamun," Rameses V "-sekheperenre," Rameses VII "-setepenre-meryamun," Rameses VIII "-akhenamun," with multiple examples during the Third Intermediate Period, also using other core prenomina.

43   Petrie 1894: 29, 42.

44   Bouriant 1893: 70–71.

45   On the prince Aakheperure, see Dodson 1990: 94.

46   Scheil 1894: 588.

47   Maspero 1896: 317 n.2.

48   Petrie 1899: 227.

49   Gauthier 1912: 344 n.2.

50   Newberry 1928: 5.

51   Petrie 1894: 38–44.

52   Winckler 1896.

53   Bouriant 1884: 2–7; this was part of work carried out since 1881 that had revealed the South Tombs, but the full results, which also covered the Royal Tomb, discovered by local inhabitants at the beginning of the decade, but not "officially" found until a decade later, did not appear until 1903 (Bouriant, Legrain, and Jéquier 1903).

54   E.g., Griffith in Petrie 1899: 215; full transcriptions and translations of all the hymns were published by Griffith and Davies in Davies 1903–1908: 6:25–35.

55   For this, and many other matters to do with the site and the period, see Montserrat 2000.

56   For an overview of work carried out by the Fund (later Society), down to the beginning of the 1980s, see Aldred 1982.

57   On the origins of the excavations, and their progress, see Matthes [2012]: 427–30 and Finneiser [2012].

58   Weigall 1910.

59   Cf. Montserrat 2000: 98–105.

60   Seyfried [2012].

61   Porter and Moss 1934: 202–203; Seyfried [2012]: 312–47[96–128].

62   A similar example of the king is Louvre E11076 (purchased in 1905; Porter and Moss 1934: 234). The idea that they were indeed "masters" is supported by the identification of plaster head Cairo JE59288 as a direct copy of the Nefertiti bust (paper presented at the British Museum by Christian Bayer, September 2019).

63   Berlin ÄM21360 (Seyfried [2012]: 334[121]).

64   For this and much of the following, see Krauss 2008; 2009: 20–21; see also Tyldesley 2018: 119–74 for an overview of the modern history of the bust.

65   For this and the immediately following, see Matthes [2012]: 431–36.

66   The Neues Museum was a building that accommodated a number of separate institutions, of which the Ägyptisches Museum was one.

67   This is today in the Huis Doorn in the Netherlands, where the deposed Kaiser lived in exile after the First World War.

68   Wildung 2013: 79. Such replicas are available at the time of writing from the Gipsformerei der Staatlichen Museen zu Berlin (€8,900 for a painted version, €1,290 for one in plain white): http://ww2.smb.museum/smb/export/downloadPM.php?id=2900

69   Cf. Savoy [2012].

70   Worms 1916; prior to this there had been just a note on a ring bearing her name (Nash 1902).

71   Muschler 1935.

72   Holmes 1959.

73   E. Wells [1964] (translated into German 1977).

74   Woolley 1922: 81–82.

75   In spite of lacking the additional cartouche necessary for such a representation: Schäfer, the first publisher of the stela (1914: 76), had followed this logic in making the pair Akhenaten and Nefertiti, as had Borchardt (1923: 9).

76   Newberry 1928: 7.

77   Newberry 1928: 7.

78   Montserrat 2000: 168–82.

79   Hayes 1959: 294.

80   Perepelkin 1968 = 1978: 58–73, seconded by J.R. Harris 1974.

81   Borchardt 1923: 32–38 (actually published in 1924); this included the first color and monochrome images to appear; his 1913 preliminary report on the excavations had merely mentioned it in passing, with a heavily cropped photograph (pl. 19) of just the face, giving the impression that it was similar to the plaster faces.

82   For this and the following, see Voss [2012].

83   Cairo JE44863, showing the royal family; it has been suggested that this may actually be a forgery (Krauss 2009).

84   An Old Kingdom figure of Ranefer and an Eighteenth Dynasty one of Amenhotep son of Hapu.

85   For this and the following, see Kischkewitz [2012].

86   On much of the wartime and postwar history of the Ägyptisches Museum, see Althoff 1998: 39–46, 61–67; on the movements of the Nefertiti bust, see also Jung [2012]: 425.

87   A new publication of the piece was prepared by Rudolf Anthes in 1954.

88   Asendorf et. al. 2009; Nys and Reichert 2009; a photographic survey of the museum prior to its rebuilding is to be found in Kilger and Maaz 2009.

89   On an abortive earlier proposed location, see Wildung 2013: 87–88.

90   Stierlin 2009; Köller 2013.

91   Huppertz et al. 2009; cf. Tyldesley 2018: 160–66.

92   J.R. Harris 1973a; he then elaborated his views in J.R. Harris 1973b; 1974b; 1977; see also Samson 1973; 1976–79; 1982a–d; 1985: 5–99.

93   E.g., Aldred 1968; 1988; Giles 1970; Tawfik 1975; 1981; Loeben 1986; Dodson 1981; 1992; 1993; 1994; 2001; 2002; 2003; 2005.

94   Krauss 1978: 43–47.

95 Allen 1988: 125–26; 1991; 1994.
96 But see Angenot's suggested alternative identities, p. 129.
97 Gabolde 1998: 153–57.
98 Cf., however, the objections of Kemp 2016.
99 E.g., Gabolde 1998: 147–226.
100 Gabolde's attempts at explaining this away do not convince.
101 Allen 2009: 19–20.
102 Allen 2016: 11.
103 Paper delivered at the Annual Meeting of the American Research Center in Egypt in Alexandria, VA, in April 2019, and subsequently reported in the popular press.
104 Based primarily on the double-crowned individual's gesture of chucking their companion under the chin, which seems otherwise only known in Amarna art carried out by daughters of Akhenaten and Nefertiti.
105 Piacentini and Orsenigo 2004: 131–32.
106 http://www.oocities.org/scribelist/do_we_have_.htm, updated in Luban 2015.
107 See summary in Reeves 1990: 204–205, 210–11.
108 James 2001.
109 J.E. Harris et al. 1979; skepticism had, however, been raised in Germer 1984.
110 Fletcher 2004: 350–80.
111 Elliot Smith had examined all three mummies in 1907 (G.E. Smith 1912: 38–42), and the Elder Lady had been X-rayed in 1967.
112 Mentioned, but not included, in Fletcher 2004, although it has appeared subsequently online, for example, https://www.standard.co.uk/news/face-of-an-ancient-beauty-6965872.html.
113 Fletcher 2004; only a small part of this actually covers the question of the identification of the mummy, with the full argumentation nowhere set out in a consolidated manner.
114 See summary and references in Rose 2004; Hawass argued that the mummy was actually male (e.g., *Sunday Times*, 22 May 2005).
115 Hawass et al. 2010.
116 Oddly, the "Boy" was not DNA-tested, and was left in KV35; as noted above, it appears to have been moved from elsewhere in the tomb, and may actually be one of the tomb's original occupants. On the other hand, Fletcher 2004: 364 suggested that X-rays showed such similarities with the Elder Lady that he could potentially be her son; likewise that the embalming methods pointed to contemporaneity with the two women. Her further suggestion that the body was that of Thutmose, eldest son of Amenhotep III, would seem unlikely, given his death a decade before Akhenaten's accession and service as high priest of Ptah, which would have suggested burial at Saqqara—and even if at Thebes, without an obvious scenario for ending up alongside the apparent Tiye and Nefertiti in KV35.
117 Dodson 2018b, which is based on the author's involvement in the making of the program; his role was, however, strictly on historical matters, and he had no input into the reconstruction other than commenting on the skin tone adopted.
118 The head was completed with the "Nefertiti crown," which has been replaced digitally in our image by a skullcap to allow better comparison with the mummy's head; it has further had the multiple ear piercings seen on the latter added.
119 https://news.nationalgeographic.com/2018/02/king-tut-tomb-hidden-chamber-scan-egypt/; see also Forbes 2018 and Burzacott 2018.
120 In the meantime Reeves has issued a restatement of his theories (Reeves 2019).
121 Marchant 2020.

BIBLIOGRAPHY

Abbreviations for Periodicals

AncEg	*Ancient Egypt* (Manchester).	JEH	*Journal of Egyptian History* (Leiden).
AO	*Acta Orientalia* (Copenhagen).	JNES	*Journal of Near Eastern Studies* (Chicago).
ASAE	*Annales du Service des antiquités de l'Égypte* (Cairo).	JSSEA	*Journal of the Society for the Study of Egyptian Antiquities* (Toronto).
BACE	*Bulletin of the Australian Centre for Egyptology* (North Ryde).	Kmt	*Kmt: A Modern Journal of Ancient Egypt* (San Francisco).
BIFAO	*Bulletin de l'Institut français d'archéologie orientale du Caire* (Cairo).	MDAIK	*Mitteilungen des Deutschen Archäologischen Instituts, Kairo* (Mainz).
BMMA	*Bulletin of the Metropolitan Museum of Art* (New York).	MDOG	*Mitteilungen der Deutschen Orient-Gesellschaft zu Berlin* (Berlin).
BSEG	*Bulletin de la Société d'Égyptologie de Genève* (Geneva).	OMRO	*Oudheidkundige Mededelingen uit het Rijksmuseum van Oudheden te Leiden* (Leiden).
BSFE	*Bulletin de la Société française d'Égyptologie* (Paris).	PSBA	*Proceedings of the Society for Biblical Archaeology* (London).
CdE	*Chronique d'Égypte* (Brussels).	RdE	*Revue d'Égyptologie* (Leuven).
EgArch	*Egyptian Archaeology: Bulletin of the Egypt Exploration Society* (London).	RecTrav	*Recueil de travaux relatifs à la philologie et à l'archéologie égyptiennes et assyriennes* (Paris).
ÉNiM	*Égypte Nilotique et Méditerranéenne* (Lyon: Université Paul Valéry)	S&N	*Sudan and Nubia: The Sudan Archaeological Society Bulletin* (London).
GM	*Göttinger Miszellen* (Göttingen).		
JAMA	*Journal of the American Medical Association* (Chicago).		
JARCE	*Journal of the American Research Center in Egypt* (New York).		
JCS	*Journal of Cuneiform Studies* (Cambridge, MA).	SAK	*Studien zur altägyptischen Kultur* (Hamburg).
JEA	*Journal of Egyptian Archaeology* (London).	ZÄS	*Zeitschrift für Ägyptische Sprache und Altertumskunde* (Leipzig & Berlin).

Works Cited

Aldred, C. 1957. "The End of the El-'Amārna Period." *JEA* 43: 30–41.

———. 1959. "The Beginning of the El-'Amārna Period." *JEA* 45: 19–33.

———. 1968. *Akhenaten, Pharaoh of Egypt.* London: Thames & Hudson.

———. 1973. *Akhenaten and Nefertiti.* New York: Viking Press.

———. 1982. "El-Amarna." In *Excavating in Egypt: The Egypt Exploration Society 1882–1982,* edited by T.G.H. James, 89–106. London: Trustees of the British Museum.

———. 1988. *Akhenaten, King of Egypt.* London: Thames & Hudson.

Allen, J.P. 1988. "Two Altered Inscriptions of the Late Amarna Period." *JARCE* 25: 117–26.

———. 1991. "Akhenaten's 'Mystery' Coregent and Successor: Were Ankhkheperure Neferneferuaten and Ankhkheperure Smenkhkare Djeserkheperure One and the Same, or Two *Different* Kings?" *Amarna Letters* 1: 74–85.

———. 1994. "Nefertiti and Smenkh-ka-re." *Göttinger Miszellen* 141: 7–17.

———. 2009. "The Amarna Succession." In *Causing His Name to Live: Studies in Egyptian Epigraphy and History in Memory of William J. Murnane,* edited by P.J. Brand and L. Cooper, 9–20. Leiden: Brill.

———. 2010. "The Original Owner of Tutankhamun's Canopic Coffins." In *Millions of Jubilees: Studies in Honor of David P. Silverman,* edited by Z. Hawass and J. Houser Wegner, 1, 27–41. Cairo: Conseil Suprême des Antiquités.

———. 2016. "The Amarna Succession Revisited." *GM* 249: 9–13.

Althoff, J. 1998. *The Ägyptisches Museum.* Berlin: Berlin Edition/Quintessenz Verlag.

Anthes, R 1954. *Die Büste der Königin Nofret Ete.* Ehemals Staatliche Museen Berlin. Berlin: Gebrüder Mann.

Arnold, Dorothea 1996. *The Royal Women of Amarna: Images of Beauty from Ancient Egypt.* New York: Metropolitan Museum of Art.

Asendorf, O., J. Haspel, N. Heuler, G. Holan, and E.M. Niemann, eds. 2009. *The Neues Museum Berlin: Conserving, Restoring, Rebuilding within the World Heritage.* Berlin: Stiftung Preussischer Kulturbesitz.

Assmann, J. 1984. *Ägypten: Theologie und Frömmigkeit einer frühen Hochkultur.* Stuttgart: Kohlhammer.

———. 1992. "Akhanyati's Theology of Light and Time." *Proceedings, Israel Academy of Sciences and Humanities,* 7/4: 143–76.

———. 1993. *Monotheismus und Kosmotheismus: Ägyptische Formen eines "Denkens des Einen" und ihre europäische Rezeptionsgeschichte.* Heidelberg: Universitätsverlag C. Winter.

Badawy, A. 1956. "Maru-Aten: Pleasure Resort or Temple?" *JEA* 42: 58–64.

Baines, J. 2003. "On the Genre and Purpose of the 'Large Commemorative Scarabs' of Amenhotep III." In *Hommages à Fayza Haikal,* 29–43. Cairo: Institut français d'archéologie orientale.

Bednarski, A. 2009. "Life after Amarna: The Post-excavation History of JE 59286." In *Beyond the Horizon: Studies in Egyptian Art, Archaeology and History in Honour of Barry J. Kemp,* edited by S. Ikram and A. Dodson, 1–8. Cairo: Supreme Council of Antiquities.

Bednarski, A., A. Dodson, and S. Ikram, eds. Forthcoming. *A History of World Egyptology.* Cambridge: Cambridge University Press.

Beinlich, H., and M. Saleh 1989. *Corpus der Hieroglyphischen Inschriften aus dem Grab des Tutanchamun.* Oxford: Griffith Institute.

Bickel, S. 2002. "Aspects et fonctions de la déification d'Amenhotep III." *BIFAO* 102: 63–90.

Bierbrier, M.L., ed. 2019. *Who Was Who in Egyptology.* 5th ed. London: Egypt Exploration Society.

Birch, S. 1851. "On a Remarkable Object of the Reign of Amenophis III." *Archaeological Journal* 8: 396–410.

Birrell, M. 1987. "Was Ay the Father of Kiya?" *BACE* 8: 11–18.

Blankenberg-van Delden, C. 1969. *The Large Commemorative Scarabs of Amenhotep III*. Leiden: E.J. Brill.

Bodziony, K. 2007. "The Amarna Technique of Composite Sculpture." *Studies in Ancient Art and Civilization* 10. Krakow. http://www.archeo.uj.edu.pl/saac/10/10.3.pdf

Borchardt, L. 1913. "Ausgrabungen in Tell el-Amarna 1912/13." *MDOG* 52: 1–55.

———. 1923. *Porträts der Königin Nofret-ete aus den Grabungen 1912/13 in Tell el-Amarna*. Leipzig: Hinrichs.

Bouriant, U. 1884. "Deux jours de fouilles à Tell el Amarna." In *Mémoires publiés par les membres de la Mission Archéologique Française au Caire* 1, 1–22. Paris: Ernest Leroux.

———. 1885. "A Thebes: II.—A propos de debris du temple d'Aten à Karnak." *RecTrav* 6: 51–55.

———. 1893. "Notes de voyage." *RecTrav* 14: 67–74.

Bouriant, U., G. Legrain, and G. Jéquier. 1903. *Monuments pour servir à l'étude du culte d'Atonou en Égypte*. Vol. 1, *Les tombes de Khouitatonou*. Cairo: Institut français d'archéologie orientale.

Breasted, J.H. 1905. *A History of Egypt from the Earliest Times to the Persian Conquest*. New York: Charles Scribner's Sons.

Breger, C. 2006. "The 'Berlin' Nefertiti Bust." In *The Body of the Queen: Gender and Rule in the Courtly World, 1500–2000*, edited by R. Schulte, 281–305. Frankfurt and New York: Berghahn Books.

Brock, E.C. 1996. "The Sarcophagus of Queen Tiy." *JSSEA* 26: 8–21.

Broschat, K., C. Eckmann, and S. Seidlmayer. 2016. "Die goldene Totenmaske des Tutanchamun: wissenschaftliche Restaurierung und Analyse." *Archäologie in Ägypten: Magazin des Deutschen Archäologischen Instituts Kairo* 4: 10–19.

Brunner, H. 1938. "Eine neue Amarna-Prinzessin." *ZÄS* 74: 104–108.

Brugsch, H. 1877. *Geschichte Aegypten's unter den Pharaonen: nach den Denkmälern*. Leipzig: Hinrichs.

———. 1879. *Egypt under the Pharaohs: A History Derived Entirely from the Monuments*. Translated by H. Danby Seymour. London: John Murray.

———. 1859. *Histoire d'Égypte dès les premiers temps de son existence jusqu'à nos jours*. Leipzig: Hinrichs.

———. 1891. *Egypt under the Pharaohs: A History Derived Entirely from the Monuments*. Edited by M. Brodrick. London: John Murray.

Bryant, A.C., and F.W. Read. 1893. "An Inscription of Khuenaten." *PSBA* 15: 206–15.

Bryce, T.R. 1990. "The Death of Niphururiya and Its Aftermath." *JEA* 76: 97–105.

Budge, E.A.W. 1902. *A History of Egypt from the End of the Neolithic Period to the Death of Cleopatra VII, B.C.* London: Kegan Paul, Trench, Trübner.

Bunsen, C.C.J. 1845–57. *Aegyptens Stelle in der Weltgeschichte*. Hamburg/Gotha: Bei Friedrich Perthes.

———. 1854. *Egypt's Place in Universal History*. Translated by C.H. Cottrell, II. London: Longman, Green, Brown & Longmans.

Buvot, J.-L. 2003. *Les serviteurs funéraires royaux et princiers de l'Ancienne Égypte*. Paris: Réunion des Musées Nationaux.

Burzacott, J. 2018. "Latest News. Tutankhamun's Tomb: The Latest Scan Results Reveal There Are No Hidden Chambers." *Nile* 14: 6–8.

Callender, G. 1998. "What Sex Was King Sobeknofru and What Is Known about Her Reign?" *Kmt* 9/1: 45–56.

Carlotti, J.-F., and P. Martinez. 2013. "Nouvelles observations architecturales et épigraphiques sur la Grande Salle Hypostyle du temple d'Amon-Rê à Karnak." *Cahiers de Karnak* 14: 231–77.

Champollion, J.-F. 1824–26. *Lettres à M. le duc de Blacas d'Aulps, Premier Gentilhomme de la Chambre, Pair de France, etc., relatives au Musée Royal Égyptien de Turin.* 2 vols. Paris: Firmin Didot. http://oeb.griffith.ox.ac.uk/ReferenceExport.aspx?id=136954.

Cottevieille-Giraudet, R. 1936. *Rapport sur les fouilles de Médamoud (1932): les reliefs d'Aménophis IV, Akhenaton.* Cairo: Institut français d'archéologie orientale.

Cross, S.W. 2008. "The Hydrology of the Valley of the Kings." *JEA* 94: 303–12.

———. 2009. "The Re-Sealing of KV62." *AncEg* 10/2: 16–22.

———. 2014. "The Workmen's Huts and Stratigraphy in the Valley of the Kings." *JEA* 100: 133–50.

Dabbs, G.R., J.C. Rose, and M. Zabecki. 2015. "The Bioarchaeology of Akhetaten: Unexpected Results from a Capital City." In *Egyptian Bioarchaeology: Humans, Animals, and the Environment*, edited by S. Ikram, J. Kaiser, and R. Walker, 43–52. Leiden: Sidestone Press.

Darnell, J.C., and C. Manassa. 2007. *Tutankhamun's Armies: Battle and Conquest during Ancient Egypt's Late 18th Dynasty.* Hoboken, NJ: John Wiley & Sons.

Davies, N. de G. 1903–1908. *The Rock Tombs of El Amarna.* 6 vol. London: Egypt Exploration Fund.

———. 1923. "The Graphic Work of the Expedition." *BMMA* 18/12, Part 2: 40–53.

———. 1941. *The Tomb of the Vizier Ramose.* London: Egypt Exploration Society.

Davis, T.M. 1910. *The Tomb of Queen Tîyi.* London: Constable.

Davis, T.W. 2019. "Field VI: The Domestic Space." In *Excavations in North Sinai: Tell el-Borg* 2, edited by J.K. Hoffmeier, 278–347. University Park, PA: Eisenbrauns.

Desroches-Noblecourt, C. 1963. *Tutankhamen: Life and Death of a Pharaoh.* London: The Connoisseur and Michael Joseph.

Dodson, A.M. 1981. "Nefertiti's Regality: A Comment." *JEA* 67: 179.

———. 1990. "Crown Prince Djhutmose and the Royal Sons of the Eighteenth Dynasty." *JEA* 76: 87–96.

———. 1992. "KV 55 and the End of the Reign of Akhenaten." *VI Congresso Internazionale di Egittologia*, 1, 135–39. Turin: n.p.

———. 1993. "On the Origin, Contents and Fate of Biban el-Moluk Tomb 55." *GM* 132: 21–28.

———. 1994. *The Canopic Equipment of the Kings of Egypt*, with contributions by Otto J. Schaden, Edwin C. Brock, and Mark Collier. London: Kegan Paul International.

———. 1996. Review of Eaton-Krauss 1993. *JEA* 82: 224–26.

———. 2001. "The Puzzle of Tomb 55." In *The Seventy Great Mysteries of the Ancient World*, edited by B.M. Fagan, 219–22. London: Thames & Hudson.

———. 2002. "The Canopic Coffinettes of Tutankhamun and the Identity of Ankhkheperure." In *Egyptian Museum Collections around the World: Studies for the Centennial of the Egyptian Museum, Cairo*, edited by M. Eldamaty and M. Trad, 1:275–85. Cairo: Supreme Council of Antiquities.

———. 2003. "Why Did Nefertiti Disappear?" In *Seventy Mysteries of Ancient Egypt*, edited by B. Manley, 127–31. London: Thames & Hudson.

———. 2005. "Akhenaten." In *Encyclopedia of African History*, edited by K. Shillington, 36–37. New York: Fitzroy Dearborn.

————. 2009. "On the Alleged 'Amenhotep III/ IV Coregency' Graffito at Meidum." *GM* 221: 25–28.

————. 2014a. *Amarna Sunrise: Egypt from Golden Age to Age of Heresy.* Cairo: American University in Cairo Press.

————. 2014b. "The Coregency Conundrum." *Kmt* 25/2: 28–35.

————. 2018a. *Amarna Sunset: Nefertiti, Tutankhamun, Ay, Horemheb, and the Egyptian Counter-Reformation.* 2nd ed. Cairo: American University in Cairo Press.

————. 2018b. "Nefertiti and the Younger Lady." *Kmt* 29/2: 26–27.

————. 2018–19. "The Royal Tomb at Amarna Revisited." *JSSEA* 45: 45–57.

————. 2019a. *Rameses III, King of Egypt: His Life and Afterlife.* Cairo: American University in Cairo Press.

————. 2019b. *Afterglow of Empire: Egypt from the Fall of the New Kingdom to the Saite Renaissance.* 2nd ed. Cairo: American University in Cairo Press.

————. 2019c. "The Myths of Tiye and Nefertiti." *Journal of History and Cultures* 10: 1–21.

————. 2020a. "On Meryetaten." In *Beloved of Seshat: Essays in Honour of Fayza Haikal,* edited by A. Omar. London: GHP.

————. 2020b. "On the Graffito in Theban Tomb 139." In *Guardian of Ancient Egypt: Essays in Honor of Zahi Hawass,* edited by J. Kamrin, M. Megahed, S. Ikram, M. Bárta, and M. Lehner. Prague: Charles University.

Dodson, A., and S. Cross. 2016. "The Valley of the Kings in the Reign of Tutankhamun." *EgArch* 48: 3–8.

Dodson, A., and D. Hilton. 2004. *The Complete Royal Families of Ancient Egypt.* London & New York: Thames & Hudson; Cairo: American University in Cairo Press.

Dorman, P.F. 2009. "The Long Coregency Revisited: Architectural and Iconographic Conundra in the Tomb of Kheruef." In *Causing His Name to Live: Studies in Egyptian Epigraphy and History in Memory of William J. Murnane,* edited by P.J. Brand and L. Cooper, 65–82. Leiden: Brill.

Eaton-Krauss, M. 1993. *The Sarcophagus in the Tomb of Tutankhamun.* Oxford: Griffith Institute.

————. 2008a. *The Thrones, Chairs, Stools, and Footstools from the Tomb of Tutankhamun.* Oxford: Griffith Institute.

————. 2008b. "Seats of Power: The Thrones of Tutankhamun." *Kmt* 19/2: 18–33.

Eaton-Krauss, M., and W.J. Murnane. 1991. "Tutankhamun, Ay, and the Avenue of Sphinxes between Pylon X and the Mut Precinct at Karnak." *BSEG* 15: 31–38.

Edel, E. 1997. *Der Vertrag zwischen Ramses II. von Ägypten und Ḫattušili III. von Ḫatti.* Berlin: Gebrüder Mann.

Edwards, I.E.S. 1972. *Treasures of Tutankhamun.* London: Michael Joseph.

Engelbach, R. 1940. "Material for a Revision of the History of the Heresy Period of the XVIIIth Dynasty." *ASAE* 40: 133–65.

Epigraphic Survey. 1980. *The Tomb of Kheruef: Theban Tomb 192.* Chicago: Oriental Institute.

Erman, A. 1900. "Geschichtlichen Inschriften aus dem Berliner Museum." *ZÄS* 38: 112–26.

Ertman, E.L. 1976. "The Cap-crown of Nefertiti: Its Function and Probable Origin." *JARCE* 13: 63–67.

————. 1992. "The Search for the Significance and Origin of Nefertiti's Tall Blue Crown." In *Sesto Congresso internazionale di egittologia: atti 1,* 189–93. Turin: International Association of Egyptologists.

————. 2003. "The Identity of the King and Queen on Tutankhamun's Golden Throne." In *Egyptology at the Dawn of the Twenty-first Century: Proceedings of the Eighth International Congress of Egyptologists, Cairo, 2000,* edited by Z. Hawass and L.P. Brock, 2:209–14. Cairo: American University in Cairo Press.

———. 2006. "Smiting the Enemy in the Reign of Akhenaten: A Family Affair." *Kmt* 17/4: 59–65.

———. 2009. "Images of Amenhotep IV and Nefertiti in the Style of the Previous Reign." In *Causing His Name to Live: Studies in Egyptian Epigraphy and History in Memory of William J. Murnane*, edited by P.J. Brand and L. Cooper, 89–94. Leiden and Boston: Brill.

Fenwick, H. 2006. "The Amarna Survey." *JEA* 92: 52–54.

Filer, J. 2000. "The KV 55 Body: The Facts." *EgArch* 17: 13–14.

———. 2002. "Anatomy of a Mummy." *Archaeology* 55/2: 26–29.

Finneiser, K. [2012]. "The Excavation Campaigns in Tell el-Amarna." In *In the Light of Amarna: 100 Years of the Nefertiti Discovery*, edited by F. Seyfried, 438–44. Berlin: Ägyptisches Museum und Papyrussamlung, Staatlich Museen zu Berlin.

Fletcher, J. 2004. *The Search for Nefertiti*. London: Hodder & Stoughton.

Forbes, D.C. 2000. "Seven Battered Osiride Figures in the Cairo Museum and the Sphinx Avenue of Tutankhamen at Karnak." *Amarna Letters* 4: 82–87.

———. 2018. "No There There: 3rd GPR-Scan of KV62 Confirms the 2nd." *Kmt* 29/3: 19–27.

Frankfort, H., and J.D.S. Pendlebury. 1933. *City of Akhenaten.* Vol. 2, *The North Suburb and the Desert Altars.* London: Egypt Exploration Society.

Freed, R.E. 1999. "Art in the Service of Religion and the State." In *Pharaohs of the Sun: Akhenaten; Nefertiti; Tutankhamen*, edited by R.E. Freed, Y.J. Markowitz, and S.H. D'Auria, 110–43. London: Thames and Hudson; Boston: Museum of Fine Arts.

Gaballa, G.A. 1977. *The Memphite Tomb Chapel of Mose.* Warminster: Aris and Phillips.

Gabolde, M. 1990. "Le droit d'aînesse d'Ankhesenpaaton (à propos de deux récents articles sur la stèle UC 410)." *BSFE* 14: 33–47.

———. 1992. "Baketaton fille de Kiya?" *BSEG* 16: 27–40.

———. 1998. *D'Akhenaton à Toutânkhamon.* Lyon: Université Lumière-Lyon 2.

———. 2013. "L'ADN de la famille royale amarnienne et les sources égyptiennes." *ÉNiM* 6: 177–203. http://www.enim-egyptologie.fr/index.php?page=enim-6&n=10.

———. 2015. *Toutankhamon.* Paris: Pygmalion.

Gardiner, A.H. 1928. "The Graffito from the Tomb of Pere." *JEA* 14: 10–11.

———. 1952. "Tuthmosis III Returns Thanks to Amun." *JEA* 38: 6–23.

Gauthier, H. 1912. *Le livre des rois d'Égypte,* vol. 2. Cairo: Institut français d'archéologie orientale.

Germer, R. 1984. "Die angebliche Mumie der Teje: Probleme interdisziplinärere Arbeiten." *SAK* 11: 85–90.

———. 2001. "Die Mumie aus dem Sarg in KV 55." In *Das Geheimnis des goldenes Sarges: Echnaton und das Ende der Amarnazeit*, edited by A. Grimm and S. Schoske, 58–61. Munich: Lipp Verlag.

Giles, F.J. 1970. *Ikhnaton: Legend and History.* London: Hutchinson.

———. 2001. *The Amarna Age: Egypt.* Warminster: Aris and Phillips.

Gliddon, G.R. 1841. *An Appeal to the Antiquaries of Europe on the Destruction of the Monuments of Egypt.* London: J. Madden.

Gohary, J. 1992. *Akhenaten's Sed-festival at Karnak.* London and New York: Kegan Paul International.

Green, L. 2000. "Crowned Heads: Royal Regalia of the Amarna and Pre- & Post-Amarna Periods." *Amarna Letters* 4: 60–75.

Grimm, A. 2001. "Ägyptologisches Kaleidoskop: Materialien zur KV 55 Diskussion." In *Das Geheimnis des goldenes Sarges: Echnaton und das Ende der Amarnazeit*, edited by A. Grimm and S. Schoske, 121–36. Munich: Lipp Verlag.

Gunn, B. 1923. "Notes on the Aten and His Names." *JEA* 9: 168–76.

Güterbock, H.G. 1956. "The Deeds of Suppiluliuma as Told by His Son, Mursili II." *JCS* 10: 41–68, 75–98, 107–30.

Györy, H. 1998. "Remarks on Amarna Amulets." In *Proceedings of the Seventh International Congress of Egyptologists, Cambridge, 3–9 September 1995*, edited by C.J. Eyre, 497–507. Leuven: Peeters.

Haas Dantes, F. 2018. "The North Wall: Meaning and Symbols." *Nile* 15: 31–43.

Habachi, L. 1958. "God's Fathers and the Role They Played in the History of the First Intermediate Period." *ASAE* 55: 167–90.

Hanke, R. 1978. *Amarna-Reliefs aus Hermopolis: Neue Veröffentlichungen und Studien*. Hildesheim: Gerstenberg Verlag.

Hari, R. 1976. "La reine d'Horemheb était-elle la soeur de Nefertiti?" *CdE* 51, no. 101: 39–46.

Haring, B.J.J. 1997. *Divine Households: Administrative and Economic Aspects of the New Kingdom Royal Memorial Temples in Western Thebes*. Leiden: Nederlands Instituut van Nabije Oosten.

Harris, J.E, and F. Hussein. 1991. "The Identification of the Eighteenth Dynasty Royal Mummies: A Biological Perspective." *International Journal of Osteoarchaeology* 1/3: 235–39.

Harris, J.E., and K.R. Weeks. 1973. *X-Raying the Pharaohs*. London: Macdonald.

Harris, J.E., E.F. Wente, C.F. Cox, I. El Nawaway, C.J. Kowalski, A.T. Storey, W.R. Russell, P.V. Ponitz, and G.F. Walker. 1979. "The Identification of the 'Elder Lady' in the Tomb of Amenhotep II as Queen Tiye." *Delaware Medical Journal* 51/2: 89–93.

Harris, J.R. 1973a. "Neferneferuaten Rediviva." *AO* 35: 5–13.

———. 1973b. "Neferneferuaten." *GM* 4: 15–17.

———. 1973c. "The Date of the 'Restoration' Stela of Tutankhamun." *GM* 5: 9–11.

———. 1974a. "Kiya." *CdE* 49: 27–30.

———. 1974b. "Neferneferuaten Regnans." *AO* 36: 11–21.

———. 1975. "Contributions to the History of the Eighteenth Dynasty." *SAK* 2: 95–101.

———. 1977. "Akhenaten or Nefertiti?" *AO* 38: 5–10.

———. 1992. "Akhenaten and Neferneferuaten." In *After Tut'ankhamūn*, edited by C.N. Reeves, 55–72. London and New York: Kegan Paul International.

———. 2004. "En sag om forveksling." *Papyrus* 24/2: 4–13.

Harrison, R.G. 1966. "An Anatomical Examination of the Pharaonic Remains Purported to Be Akhenaten." *JEA* 52: 95–119.

Hawass, Z., Y.Z. Gad, S. Ismail, R. Khairat, D. Fathalla, N. Hasan, A. Ahmed, H. Elleithy, M. Ball, F. Gaballah, S. Wasef, M. Fateen, H. Amer, P. Gostner, A. Selim, A. Zink, and C.M. Pusch. 2010. "Ancestry and Pathology in King Tutankhamun's Family." *JAMA* 303/7: 638–47.

Hawass, Z., and S.N. Saleem. 2016. *Scanning the Pharaohs: CT Imaging of the New Kingdom Royal Mummies*. Cairo: American University in Cairo Press.

Hayes, W.C. 1951. "Inscriptions from the Palace of Amenhotep III." *JNES* 10: 35–56, 82–112, 156–83, 231–42.

———. 1959. *The Scepter of Egypt*, vol. 2. New York: Metropolitan Museum of Art.

Helck, W. 1955–58. *Urkunden der 18. Dynastie*, 17–22. Berlin: Akademie-Verlag.

———. 1984. "Kijê." *MDAIK* 40: 159–67.

Hincks, E. 1848. "On the Defacement of Divine and Royal Names on Egyptian Monuments." *Transactions of the Royal Irish Academy* 21: 105–13.

Hoffmeier, J.K., and J. van Dijk. 2010. "New Light on the Amarna Period from North Sinai." *JEA* 96: 191–205.

Holmes, W. 1959. *She Was Queen of Egypt: Hatshepsut, Nefertiti, Cleopatra, Shagaret el Dor.* London: G. Bell.

Hornung, E. 1999. *Akhenaten and the Religion of Light.* Translated by D. Lorton. Ithaca, NY: Cornell University Press.

Huber, M.T. 2016. *Who Was the Father of Tutankhamun?* Hamburg: Books on Demand.

———. 2018. "The North Wall Tutankhamun KV 62, Part I: The New Interpretation." *Nile* 14: 9–23.

———. 2019a. "The Mother of Tutankhamen: Not Nefertiti but Meritaten." *Kmt* 30/1: 18–28.

———. 2019b. "The Enigmatic Mummy from KV55, Part 2." *Nile Magazine* 21: 19–29.

Huppertz, A., D. Wildung, B.J. Kemp, T. Nentwig, P. Asbach, F.M. Rasche, and B. Hamm. 2009. "Nondestructive Insights into Composition of the Sculpture of Egyptian Queen Nefertiti with CT." *Radiology* 251/1: 233–40.

Hussein, F., and J.E. Harris. 1988. "The Skeletal Remains from Tomb No 55." In *Fifth International Congress of Egyptology, October 29–November 3, Cairo 1988: Abstracts of Papers*, edited by A. Cherif, 140–41. Cairo: Egyptian Antiquities Organization.

Ikram, S. 1989. "Domestic Shrines and the Cult of the Royal Family at el-'Amarna." *JEA* 75: 89–101.

James, S.E. 2001. "Who Is the Mummy The Elder Lady?" *Kmt* 12/2: 42–50.

Johnson, W.R. 1996. "Amenhotep III and Amarna: Some New Considerations." *JEA* 82: 65–82.

———. 1998. "Monuments and Monumental Art under Amenhotep III." In *Amenhotep III: Perspectives on His Reign*, edited by D.B. Connor and E.H. Cline, 63–94. Ann Arbor: University of Michigan Press.

———. 2009. "Tutankhamen-Period Battle Narratives at Luxor." *Kmt* 20/4: 20–33.

———. 2012–13. "Same Statues, Different King." *Kmt* 23/4: 49–53.

———. 2015. "An Amarna Royal Head at Hanover's Museum August Kestner: Evidence for King Ankhkheperure Neferneferuaten." *Kmt* 26/3: 22–29.

———. 2017. "An Indurated-limestone Sphinx Fragment of Nefertiti in the Luxor Temple Blockyard." In *Essays for the Library of Seshat: Studies Presented to Janet H. Johnson on the Occasion of Her 70th Birthday*, edited by R.K. Ritner, 75–80. Chicago: Oriental Institute.

———. 2018. "Fresh Evidence for an Akhenaten/Nefertiti Coregency: A Talatat Block from Hermopolis with a New Join." *Kmt* 29/1: 71–76.

Jung, M. [2012]. "100 Years of the Discovery of Nefertiti." In *In the Light of Amarna: 100 Years of the Nefertiti Discovery*, edited by F. Seyfried, 421–26. Berlin: Ägyptisches Museum und Papyrussamlung, Staatlich Museen zu Berlin.

Kawai, N. 2013. "Some Remarks on the Funerary Equipment from the Tomb of Amenhotep III (KV 22)." In *Archaeological Research in the Valley of the Kings and Ancient Thebes: Papers Presented in Honor of Richard H. Wilkinson*, edited by P.P. Creaseman, 149–72. [Tucson]: University of Arizona Egyptian Expedition.

Kemp, B.J. 1995. "Outlying Temples at Amarna." In *Amarna Reports 6*, edited by B.J. Kemp, 411–62. London: Egypt Exploration Society.

———. 2008–2009. "The Amarna Project: Why Amarna Died." *AncEg* 9/3: 44–51.

———. 2012. *The City of Akhenaten and Nefertiti: Amarna and Its People.* London: Thames and Hudson.

———. 2016. "Ranefer's Sovereign: Who Was the Last Ruler at Amarna?" *Akhetaten Sun* 22/1: 13–31.

Kemp, B., ed. 2017. "Tell el-Amarna, Spring 2017." *JEA* 103: 137–51.

Kemp, B.J., and S. Garfi. 1993. *A Survey of the Ancient City of el-'Amarna.* London: Egypt Exploration Society.

Kemp, B., and J.C. Rose. 2016. "Tell el-Amarna, 2016." *JEA* 102: 1–11.

Kemp, B., and A. Stevens. 2010. *Busy Lives at Amarna: Excavations in the Main City (Grid 12 and the House of Ranefer, N49.18).* 2 vols. London: Egypt Exploration Society.

Kemp, B., A. Stevens, G.R. Dabbs, M. Zabecki, and J.C. Rose. 2013. "Life, Death and Beyond in Akhenaten's Egypt: Excavating the South Tombs Cemetery at Amarna." *Antiquity* 87/335: 64–78.

El-Khouly, A., and G.T. Martin. 1987. *Excavations in the Royal Necropolis at El-'Amarna 1984.* Cairo: Egyptian Antiquities Organization.

Kilger, A., and B. Maaz. 2009. *Das Neue Museum, Berlin: Der Bauzustand um 1990.* Berlin: Deutsche Kunstverlag.

Kischkewitz, H. [2012]. "The Thirties—Trouble with Nefertiti." In *In the Light of Amarna: 100 Years of the Nefertiti Discovery*, edited by F. Seyfried, 460–68. Berlin: Ägyptisches Museum und Papyrussamlung, Staatlich Museen zu Berlin.

Köller, Klaus. 2013. *Berlin ÄMP 21300: eine Autopsie.* Berlin: Klaus Köller.

Kozloff, A.P. 2010. "Chips Off the Old Block: Amenhotep IV's Sandstone Colossi, Re-cut from Statues of Amenhotep III." In *Millions of Jubilees: Studies in Honor of David P. Silverman*, edited by Z. Hawass and J. Houser Wegner, 1:279–94. Cairo: Supreme Council of Antiquities.

———. 2012. "Chips Off Old Statues: Carving the Amenhotep IV Colossi at Karnak." *Kmt* 23/3: 18–32.

Kramer, A. 2003. "Enigmatic Kiya." In *A Delta-man in Yebu*, edited by A.K. Eyma and C.J. Bennett, 48–63. Boca Raton, FL: Universal Publishers.

Krauss, R. 1978. *Das Ende der Amarnazeit.* Hildesheim: Gerstenberg.

———. 2008. "Why Nefertiti Went to Berlin: As Result of Division of 1912 Finds in the Thutmose Workshop at El Amarna by Ludwig Borchardt and Gustav Lefebvre." *Kmt* 19/3: 44–53.

———. 2009. "Nefertiti's Final Secret: Did Cairo Receive a Modern Forgery in Exchange for the Bust of the Queen?" *Kmt* 20/2: 18–28.

———. 2019. "Zu Henri Stierlins Thesen über die Berliner Nofretete-Büste." *GM* 257: 195–206.

Lauffray, J. 1980. "Les 'talatat' du IXe pylône et le Teny-Menou (assemblage et première reconstruction d'une paroi du temple d'Aton dans le musée de Louqsor)." *Cahiers de Karnak* 6: 67–89.

Lefébure, E. 1891. "Sur différents mots et noms égyptiens." *PSBA* 13: 470–83.

Lepsius, C.R. 1849–59. *Denkmaeler aus Aegypten und Aethiopien.* 6 vol. Berlin and Leipzig: Nicolaische Buchandlung.

———. 1851. *Über den ersten ägyptischen Götterkreis und seine geschichtlich-mythologische Entstehung.* Berlin: Bei Wilhelm Herz.

———. 1853. *Letters from Egypt, Ethiopia, and the Peninsula of Sinai.* Translated by L. and J.B. Horner. London: Henry G. Bohn.

———. 1897. *Denkmaeler aus Aegypten und Aethiopien, Text.* Edited by E. Naville, L. Borchardt, and K. Sethe. Leipzig: J.C. Hinrichs.

L'Hôte, N. 1840. *Lettres écrites d'Egypte en 1838 et 1839.* Paris: Firmin Didot.

Loeben, C.E. 1986. "Eine Bestattung der *großen königlichen Gemahlin Nofretete* in Amarna." *MDAIK* 42: 99–107.

———. 1991. "'No Evidence of Coregency': Zwei getilgte Inschriften aus dem Grab von Tutanchamun." *BSEG* 15: 82–90.

———. 1994a. "No Evidence of Coregency: Two Erased Inscriptions from Tutankhamun's Tomb." *Amarna Letters* 3: 105–109.

———. 1994b. "Nefertiti's Pillars: A Photo Essay of the Queen's Monument at Karnak." *Amarna Letters* 3: 41–45.

———. 1999. "Une inhumation de la grande épouse royale Néfertiti à Amarna? La figurine funéraire de Néfertiti." *Égypte, Afrique et Orient* 13: 25–30.

Lorenzen, E.D., and E. Willerslev. 2010. "King Tutankhamun's Family and Demise." *JAMA* 303/24: 2471.

Luban, M. 2015. *My Quest for Nefertiti*. San Antonio: Pacific Moon.

Málek, J. 1996. "The 'Coregency Relief' of Akhenaten and Smenkhkare from Memphis." In *Studies in Honor of William Kelly Simpson*, edited by P. Der Manuelian, 2:553–59. Boston: Museum of Fine Arts.

Mallinson, M. 1989. "Report on the 1987 Investigation of the Small Aten Temple." In *Amarna Reports* 5, edited by B.J. Kemp, 115–42. London: Egypt Exploration Society.

Manniche, L. 1975. "The Wife of Bata." *GM* 18: 33–38.

———. 2010. *The Akhenaten Colossi of Karnak*. Cairo: American University in Cairo Press.

Marchant, J. 2011. "Curse of the Pharaoh's DNA." *Nature* 472: 404–406.

———. 2013. *The Shadow King: The Bizarre Afterlife of King Tut's Mummy*. Boston: Da Capo Press.

———. 2020. "Is This Nefertiti's Tomb? Radar Clues Reignite Debate over Hidden Chambers: A New Survey Hints at a Previously Unknown Space beyond Tutankhamun's Burial Chamber." *Nature*, 19 February 2020. doi: 10.1038/d41586-020-00465-y

Mariette, A. 1855. "Renseignements sur les soixante-quatre Apis trouvés dans les souterrains du Sérapéum." *Bulletin archéologique de l'Athenaeum français* 1: 45–100.

———. 1874. *Aperçu de l'histoire d'Egypte*. Cairo: A. Mourès.

Martin, G.T. 1974, 1989. *The Royal Tomb at el-'Amarna* 1, 2. London: Egypt Exploration Society.

———. 2009. "The Co-regency Stela University College London 410." In *Sitting beside Lepsius: Studies in Honour of Jaromir Málek at the Griffith Institute*, edited by D. Magee, J. Bourriau, and S. Quirke, 343–59. Leuven: Peeters.

Maspero, G. 1896. *Struggle of the Nations: Egypt, Syria and Assyria*. London: Society for Promoting Christian Knowledge.

———. 1907. "Notice on Iouiya and Touiyou." In *The Tomb of Iouiya and Touiyou*, edited by T.M. Davis, xiii–xxi. London: Constable.

Matić, U. 2017. "'Her Striking but Cold Beauty': Gender and Violence in Depictions of Queen Nefertiti Smiting the Enemies." In *Archaeologies of Gender and Violence*, edited by U. Matić and B. Jensen, 103–21. Oxford: Oxbow Books.

Matthes, O. [2012]. "Ludwig Borchardt, James Simon and the Colourful Nefertiti Bust in the First Year after Her Discovery." In *In the Light of Amarna: 100 Years of the Nefertiti Discovery*, edited by F. Seyfried, 427–37. Berlin: Ägyptisches Museum und Papyrussamlung, Staatlich Museen zu Berlin.

Maystre, C. 1992. *Les grands prêtres de Ptah de Memphis*. Freiburg: Universitätsverlag; Göttingen: Vandenhoeck & Ruprecht.

McLeod, W. 1970. *Composite Bows from the Tomb of Tut'ankhamūn*. Oxford: Griffith Institute.

Montserrat, D. 2000. *Akhenaten: History, Fantasy and Ancient Egypt*. London and New York: Routledge.

Moran, W.L. 1992. *The Amarna Letters*. Baltimore: Johns Hopkins University Press.

Morkot, R.G. 1986. "Violent Images of Queenship and the Royal Cult." *Wepwawet* 2: 1–9.

Moseley, S. 2009. *Amarna: The Missing Evidence*. Calshot: Peach Pixel.

Moursi, M.I. 1972. *Die Hohenpriester des Sonnengottes von der Frühzeit Ägyptens bis zum Ende des Neuen Reiches*. Berlin: Deutscher Kunstverlag.

Murnane, W.J. 1976. "On the Accession Date of Akhenaten." In *Studies in Honor of George R. Hughes: January 12, 1977*, 163–67. Chicago: Oriental Institute of the University of Chicago.

———. 1977. *Ancient Egyptian Coregencies*. Chicago: Oriental Institute.

———. 1990. *The Road to Kadesh: A Historical Interpretation of the Battle Reliefs of King Sety I at Karnak*. 2nd ed. Chicago: Oriental Institute.

———. 1995. *Texts from the Amarna Period in Egypt*. Atlanta, GA: Scholars Press.

Murnane, W.J., and C.C. van Siclen III. 1993. *The Boundary Stelae of Akhenaten*. London and New York: Kegan Paul International.

Muschler, R.C. 1935. *Nofretete: Novelle*. Berlin: Neff.

Nash, W.L. 1902. "A Ring of Nefer-ti-ti." *PSBA* 24: 309.

Newberry, P.E. 1928. "Akhenaten's Eldest Son-in-Law 'Ankhkheprurē.'" *JEA* 14: 3–9.

Nicholson. c. 1870. "On Some Remains of the Disk Worshippers Discovered at Memphis." *Transactions of the Royal Society of Literature*, 2nd series, 9: 197–214.

Nims, C.F. 1973. "The Transition from the Traditional to the New Style of Wall Relief under Amenhotep IV." *JNES* 32: 181–87.

Nys, R., and M. Reichert, eds. 2009. *Neues Museum Berlin*. Cologne: Walther König.

Ockinga, B.G. 1997. *A Tomb from the Reign of Tutankhamun at Akhmim*. Warminster: Aris & Phillips.

Pamminger, P. 1993. "Zur Göttlichkeit Amenophis' III." *BSFE* 17: 83–92.

Panagiotakopulu, E. 2004. "Pharaonic Egypt and the Origins of Plague." *Journal of Biogeography* 31: 269–75.

Pasquali, S. 2007. "La date du papyrus BM 10056." *RdE* 58: 71–85.

———. 2011. "A Sun-shade Temple of Princess Ankhesenpaaten in Memphis?" *JEA* 97: 216–22.

Peet, T.E., and C.L. Woolley. 1923. *City of Akhenaten*. Vol. 1, *Excavations of 1921 and 1923 at El-'Amarneh*. London: Egypt Exploration Society.

Pendlebury, J.D.S. 1933. "Preliminary Report of the Excavations at Tell el-'Amarnah, 1932–3." *JEA* 19: 113–18.

———. 1951. *City of Akhenaten*. Vol. 3, *The Central City and Official Quarters*. London: Egypt Exploration Society.

Perepelkin, Yu. 1968. *Тайна золотого гроба*. Moscow: Nauka.

———. 1978. *The Secret of the Gold Coffin*. Moscow: Nauka.

Perring, J.S. 1843. "On Some Fragments from the Ruins of a Temple at El Tell." *Transactions of the Royal Society of Literature* 2nd ser., 1: 140–48.

Petrie, W.M.F. 1894. *Tell el Amarna*. London: Methuen.

———. 1899. *A History of Egypt during the XVIIth and XVIIIth Dynasties*. 3rd ed. London: Methuen.

Phillips, J. 2004. "How to Build a Body without One: Composite Statues from Amarna." In *Invention and Innovation: The Social Context of Technological Change*, vol. 2, *Egypt, the Aegean and the Near East, 1650–1150 BC. Proceedings of a Conference Held at the McDonald Institute for Archaeological Research, Cambridge, 4–6 September 2002*, edited by J. Bourriau and J. Phillips, 200–14. Oxford: Oxbow Books.

Piacentini, P., and C. Orsenigo. 2004. *La Valle dei Re Riscoperta: i giornali scavo di Victor Loret (1898–1899) e altri inediti*. Milan: Università degli Studi di Milano/Skira.

Porter, B., and R.L.B. Moss. 1934. *Topographical Bibliography of Ancient Egyptian Hieroglyphic Texts, Reliefs and Paintings*, vol. 4, *Lower and Middle Egypt*. Oxford: Clarendon Press.

———. 1937. *Topographical Bibliography of Ancient Egyptian Hieroglyphic Texts, Reliefs and Paintings*, vol. 5, *Upper Egypt: Sites*. Oxford: Clarendon Press.

———. 1939. *Topographical Bibliography of Ancient Egyptian Hieroglyphic Texts, Reliefs and Paintings*, vol. 6, *Upper Egypt: Chief Temples (excl. Thebes)*. Oxford: Clarendon Press.

———. 1952. *Topographical Bibliography of Ancient Egyptian Hieroglyphic Texts, Reliefs and Paintings*, vol. 7, *Nubia, Deserts, and Outside Egypt*. Oxford: Clarendon Press/Griffith Institute.

———. 1960–64. *Topographical Bibliography of Ancient Egyptian Hieroglyphic Texts, Reliefs and Paintings*, vol. 1, *The Theban Necropolis*. 2nd ed. Oxford: Clarendon Press/Griffith Institute.

———. 1972. *Topographical Bibliography of Ancient Egyptian Hieroglyphic Texts, Reliefs and Paintings*, vol. 2, *Theban Temples*. 2nd ed. Oxford: Griffith Institute.

———. 1974–81. *Topographical Bibliography of Ancient Egyptian Hieroglyphic Texts, Reliefs and Paintings*, vol. 3, *Memphis*. 2nd ed. by J. Málek. Oxford: Griffith Institute.

Prisse d'Avennes, E. 1843. "Remarks on the Ancient Materials of the Propyla at Karnak." *Transactions of the Royal Society of Literature*, 2nd ser., 1: 76–92.

———. 1847. *Monuments égyptiens, bas-reliefs, peintures, inscriptions, etc.* Paris: Didot.

———. 1878–79. *Histoire de l'art égyptien d'après les monuments depuis les temps les plus reculés jusqu'à la domination romaine*. Paris: Arthus Bertrand.

Quiring, H. 1960. "Die Abkunft des Tutanchamon (1358–1351)." *Klio* 38: 53–61.

Rammant Peeters, A. 1985. "Les couronnes de Nefertiti à el-Amarna." *Orientalia Lovaniensia Periodica* 16: 21–48.

Ranke, H. 1935. *Die ägyptischen Personennamen*. Vol. 1, *Verzeichnis der Namen*. Glückstadt: J.J. Augustin.

Raven, M.J. 1994. "A Sarcophagus for Queen Tiy and Other Fragments from the Royal Tomb at Amarna." *OMRO* 74: 7–20.

Redford, D.B. 1967. *History and Chronology of the Eighteenth Dynasty of Egypt: Seven Studies*. Toronto: University of Toronto Press.

———. 1973. "Studies on Akhenaten at Thebes, I: A Report on the Work of the Akhenaten Temple Project of the University Museum, University of Pennsylvania." *JARCE* 10: 77–94.

———. 1975. "Studies on Akhenaten at Thebes, II: A Report on the Work of the Akhenaten Temple Project of the University Museum, the University of Pennsylvania, for the Year 1973–4." *JARCE* 12: 9–18.

———. 1984. *Akhenaten: The Heretic King*. Princeton, NJ: Princeton University Press.

———, ed. 1988. *The Akhenaten Temple Project*. Vol. 2, *Rwd-mnw, Foreigners and Inscriptions*. Toronto: The Akhenaten Temple Project.

———. 1994. "East Karnak and the Sed-Festival of Akhenaten." In *Hommages à Jean Leclant*, vol. 1, *Études pharaoniques*, edited by C. Berger, G. Clerc, and N. Grimal, 485–92. Cairo: Institut français d'archéologie orientale.

Reeves, C.N. 1978. "A Further Occurrence of Nefertiti as ḥmt nsw ʿ3t." *GM* 30: 61–69.

———. 1988. "New Light on Kiya from Texts in the British Museum." *JEA* 74: 91–101.

———. 1990. *Valley of the Kings: The Decline of a Royal Necropolis*. London and New York: Kegan Paul International.

———. 2015. *The Burial of Nefertiti?* Tucson: Amarna Royal Tombs Project/University of Arizona Egyptian Expedition.

———. 2016. "Tutankhamun's Mask Reconsidered." In *Valley of the Kings since Howard Carter: Proceedings of the Luxor Symposium November 4, 2009*, edited by H. Elleithy, 117–34. Cairo: Ministry of Antiquities.

———. 2019. *The Decorated North Wall in the Tomb of Tutankhamun (KV 62) (The Burial of Nefertiti? II)*. Tucson: Amarna Royal Tombs Project/University of Arizona Egyptian Expedition.

Ridley, R.T. 2019. *Akhenaten: A Historian's View.* Cairo: American University in Cairo Press.

Rilly, C. 2018. "The QSAP Programme on the Temple of Queen Tiye at Sedeinga." *S&N* 22: 55–64.

Robins, G. 1983. "A Critical Examination of the Theory that the Right to the Throne of Ancient Egypt Passed through the Female Line in the 18th Dynasty." *GM* 62: 68–69.

———. 1984. "The Proportions of Figures in the Decoration of the Tombs of Tutankhamun (KV 62) and Ay (KV 23)." *GM* 72: 27–32.

———. 1987. "The Role of the Royal Family in the 18th Dynasty Up to the Reign of Amenhotpe III: 2. Royal Children." *Wepwawet* 3: 15–17.

Roeder, G. 1969. *Amarna-Reliefs aus Hermopolis: Ausgrabungen der Deutschen Hermopolis-Expedition in Hermopolis 1929–1939.* Vol. 2. Hildesheim: Gebrüder Gerstenberg.

Roehrig, C.H., ed. 2005. *Hatshepsut: From Queen to Pharaoh.* New York: Metropolitan Museum of Art.

Rose, M. 2004. "Where's Nefertiti?" *Archaeology Archive: Online Reviews.* https://archive.archaeology.org/online/reviews/nefertiti/.

Ryholt, K.S.B. 2000. "The Late Old Kingdom in the Turin King List and the Identity of Nitokris." *ZÄS* 127: 87–100.

Sadowska, M. 2000. "Semenchkare and Zannanza." *GM* 175: 73–77.

Samson, J. 1973. "Royal Inscriptions from Amarna." *CdE* 48: 243–50.

———. 1976. "Royal Names in Amarna History: The Historical Development of Nefertiti's Names and Titles." *CdE* 51: 30–38.

———. 1977. "Nefertiti's Regality." *JEA* 63: 88–97.

———. 1978. *Amarna, City of Akhenaton and Nefertiti: Nefertiti as Pharaoh.* Warminster: Aris & Phillips.

———. 1979. "Akhenaten's Successor." *GM* 32: 53–58.

———. 1982a. "Akhenaten's Coregent Ankhkheprure-Nefernefruaten." *GM* 53: 51–54.

———. 1982b. "Akhenaten's Coregent and Successor." *GM* 57: 57–59.

———. 1982c. "Nefernefruaten-Nefertiti 'Beloved of Akhenaten,' Ankhkheprure Nefernefruaten 'Beloved of Akhenaten,' Ankhkheprure Smenkhkare 'Beloved of the Aten.'" *GM* 57: 61–67.

———. 1982d. "The History of the Mystery of Akhenaten's Successor." In *L'Égyptologie en 1979: Axes prioritaires de recherches*, vol. 2, 291–97. Paris: Centre National de la Recherche Scientifique.

———. 1985. *Nefertiti and Cleopatra: Queen-Monarchs of Ancient Egypt.* London: Rubicon Press.

Savoy, B. [2012]. "Futurists, Bow Your Heads! Amarna Fever in Berlin, 1913/14." In *In the Light of Amarna: 100 Years of the Nefertiti Discovery*, edited by F. Seyfried, 452–59. Berlin: Ägyptisches Museum und Papyrussamlung, Staatlich Museen zu Berlin.

Schäfer, H. 1914. "Kunstwerke aus der Zeit Amenophis' IV." *ZÄS* 52: 73–87.

Scheil, V. 1894. *Tombeaux thébains de Mâi, des Graveurs, Rat'eserkasenb, Pârj, Djanni, Apoui, Montou-m-hat, Aba.* Paris: Ernest Leroux.

Schiff Giorgini, M. 1965, 1998–2003. *Soleb*, vols. 1, 3–5. Florence: Sansoni; Cairo: Institut français d'archéologie orientale.

Seipel, W. 1980 *Untersuchungen zu den ägyptischen Königinnen der Frühzeit und des Alten Reiches.* Hamburg: n.p.

Sethe, K. 1905. "Die Schwägerin Amenophis' IV." *ZÄS* 42: 134–35.

Seyfried, F. [2012]. "The Workshop Complex of Thutmosis." In *In the Light of Amarna: 100 Years of the Nefertiti Discovery*, edited by F. Seyfried, 170–86. Berlin: Ägyptisches Museum und Papyrussamlung, Staatlich Museen zu Berlin.

———, ed. [2012]; *In the Light of Amarna: 100 Years of the Nefertiti Discovery.* Berlin: Ägyptisches Museum und Papyrussamlung, Staatlich Museen zu Berlin.

Shannon, E. 1987. "Ring Bezels with Royal Names at the Workmen's Village 1979–1986." In *Amarna Reports*, vol. 4, edited by B.J. Kemp, 154–59. London: Egypt Exploration Society.

Sharpe, S. 1859. *A History of Egypt, from the Earliest Times till the Conquest by the Arabs A.D. 640.* London: Edward Moxon & Co.

Shaw, I. 1984. "Ring Bezels at Amarna." In *Amarna Reports*, edited by B.J. Kemp, 1:124–32. London: Egypt Exploration Society.

Smith, G.E. 1912. *The Royal Mummies.* Cairo: Institut français d'archéologie orientale.

Smith, H.S. 1976. *The Fortress of Buhen: The Inscriptions.* London: Egypt Exploration Society.

Smith, R.W., and D.B. Redford. 1976. *The Akhenaten Temple Project.* Vol. 1, *Initial Discoveries.* Warminster: Aris & Phillips.

Smith, S.T. 1992. "Intact Tombs of the 17th and 18th Dynasties from Thebes and the New Kingdom Burial System." *MDAIK* 48: 193–231.

Stannish, S.M. 2007. "Evidence for a Co-regency between Amunhotep III and Akhenaten in the Earlier Proclamation of Amarna Boundary Stelae K, X, and M." *JSSEA* 34: 159–62.

Stempel, R. 2007. "Identification of Nibhururiya and the Synchronism in the Egyptian and Hittite Chronology in the Light of Newly Reconstructed Hittite Text." *GM* 213: 97–100.

Stevens, A., G.R. Dabbs, C. Rogge, P. Rose, A. Mérat, J. Bos, J. Williamson, A. Garnett, L. Skinner, J. Dawson, A. Bettum, A. Clapham, and G. Tully. 2018. "Tell el-Amarna, Autumn 2017 and Spring 2018." *JEA* 104: 122–44.

Stewart, H.M. 1976. *Egyptian Stelae, Reliefs and Paintings from the Petrie Collection.* Vol. 1, *The New Kingdom.* Warminster: Aris & Phillips.

Stierlin, H. 2009. *Le buste de Néfertiti: Une imposture de l'égyptologie?* Gollion: InFolio.

Strouhal, E. 2010. "Biological Age of Skeletonized Mummy from Tomb KV 55 at Thebes." *Anthropologie* 48/2: 97–112.

Strudwick, N. 1985. *The Administration of Egypt in the Old Kingdom: The Highest Titles and Their Holders.* London: Kegan Paul International.

Tawfik, Sayed. 1975. "Aton Studies 3: Back Again to Nefer-nefru-Aton." *MDAIK* 31: 159–68.

———. 1981. "Aton Studies 6: Was Nefernefruaten the Immediate Successor of Akhenaten?" *MDAIK* 37: 469–73.

Theis, C. 2011. "Der Brief der Königin Daḫamunzu an den hetitischen König Šuppiluliuma I. im Lichte von Reisegeschwindigkeit und Zeitabläufen." In *Identities and Societies in the Ancient East–Mediterranean Regions: Comparative Approaches. Henning Graf Reventlow Memorial Volume Kämmerer*, edited by R. Thomas, 301–31. Münster: Ugarit-Verlag.

Thomas, A.P. 1982. "Some Palimpsest Fragments from the Maru-Aten at Amarna." *CdE* 57/113: 5–13.

Thompson, J. 1992. *Sir Gardner Wilkinson and His Circle.* Austin: University of Texas Press.

———. 2014–19. *Wonderful Things: A History of Egyptology.* 3 vols. Cairo: American University in Cairo Press.

Thompson, K. 2004. "Amarna Statuary Fragments." *EgArch* 25: 14–16.

———. 2006. "A Shattered Granodiorite Dyad of Akhenaten and Nefertiti from Tell el-Amarna." *JEA* 92: 141–51.

———. [2012]. "New Forms of Composition— Composite Statues." In *In the Light of Amarna: 100 Years of the Nefertiti Discovery*, edited by F. Seyfried, 164–69. Berlin: Ägyptisches Museum und Papyrussamlung, Staatlich Museen zu Berlin.

Traunecker, C. 1986. "Aménophis IV et Néfertiti: le couple royal d'après les talatates du IXe pylône de Karnak." *BSFE* 107: 17–44.

Troy, L. 1986. *Patterns of Queenship in Ancient Egyptian Myth and History.* Uppsala: Boreas.

Tyldesley, J. 1998, 2005. *Nefertiti: Egypt's Sun Queen.* London: Viking.

———. 2018. *Nefertiti's Face: The Creation of an Icon.* London: Profile Books.

van der Perre, A. 2014. "The Year 16 Graffito of Akhenaten in Dayr Abu Hinnis: A Contribution to the Study of the Later Years of Nefertiti." *JEH* 7: 67–108.

van de Walle, B. 1976. "La découverte d'Amarna et d'Akhenaton." *RdE* 28: 7–24.

Vandenberg, P. 1975. *Nofretete: Eine archäologische Biographie.* [Berne and Munich:] Scherz Verlag.

van Dijk, J. 1997. "The Noble Lady of Mitanni and Other Royal Favourites of the Eighteenth Dynasty." In *Essays on Ancient Egypt in Honour of Hermann te Velde*, edited by J. van Dijk, 33–46. Groningen: Styx Publications.

———. 2008. "A Colossal Statue Base of Nefertiti and Other Early Atenist Monuments from the Precinct of the Goddess Mut in Karnak." In *Servant of Mut: Studies in Honor of Richard A. Fazzini*, edited by S. D'Auria, 246–61. Leiden: Brill.

———. 2009. "The Death of Meketaten." In *Causing His Name to Live: Studies in Egyptian Epigraphy and History in Memory of William J. Murnane*, edited by P.J. Brand and L. Cooper, 83–88. Leiden: Brill.

Vergnieux, R. 1999. *Recherches sur les monuments thébains d'Amenhotep IV à l'aide d'outils informatiques: Méthodes et résultats.* Geneva: Société d'Égyptologie.

Vishnoi, V. 2000. "What Ailed Akhenaten and His Daughters?" *Amarna Letters* 4: 76–81.

Voss, S. [2012]. "The 1925 Demand for the Return of the Nefertiti Bust, a German Perspective." In *In the Light of Amarna: 100 Years of the Nefertiti Discovery*, edited by F. Seyfried, 460–68. Berlin: Ägyptisches Museum und Papyrussammlung, Staatlich Museen zu Berlin.

Waddell, W.G., trans. 1940. *Manetho.* Cambridge, MA: Harvard University Press; London: William Heinemann.

Weatherhead, F. 2007. *Amarna Palace Paintings.* London: Egypt Exploration Society.

Wegner, J. 2017. *The Sunshade Chapel of Meritaten from the House-of-Waenre of Akhenaten.* Philadelphia: University of Pennsylvania Museum of Archaeology and Anthropology.

Weigall, A.E.P. 1910. *The Life and Times of Akhnaton, Pharaoh of Egypt.* London: W. Blackwood & Sons.

Wells, E. 1964. *Nefertiti.* London: Robert Hale.

Wells, R.A. 1987. "The Amarna M, X, K Boundary Stelae Date: A Modern Calendar Equivalent." *SAK* 14: 313–33.

———. 1989. "The Amarna M, X, K Boundary Stelae Date: Ḥwt-itn Ceremonial Altar. Initial Results of a New Survey." *SAK* 16: 289–327.

Werner, E.K. 1979. "Identification of Nefertiti in *Talatat* Reliefs Previously Published as Akhenaten." *Orientalia* 48: 324–31.

Whittemore, T. 1926. "The Excavations at El-'Amarnah, Season 1924–5." *JEA* 12: 3–12.

Wiedemann, A. 1895. "Inscriptions from the Time of Amenophis IV." *PSBA* 17: 152–57.

Wildung, D. 1998. "Le frère aîné d'Ekhnaton: réflexions sur un décès prématuré." *BSFE* 143: 10–18.

———. 2013. *The Many Faces of Nefertiti.* Ostfildern: Hatje Cantz.

Wilkinson, J.G. 1828–30. *Materia Hieroglyphica: Containing the Egyptian Pantheon, and the Succession of the Pharaohs, from the Earliest Times to the Conquest by Alexander, and Other Hieroglyphical Subjects.* Malta: Government Press.

———. 1830. *Extracts from Several Hieroglyphical Subjects Found at Thebes and Other Parts of Egypt.* Malta: Government Press.

———. 1841. *Manners and Customs of the Ancient Egyptians.* 2nd series, vol. 1. London: John Murray.

———. 1854. *A Popular Account of the Ancient Egyptians.* London: John Murray.

Williamson, J. 2016. *Nefertiti's Sun Temple: A New Cult Complex at Tell El-Amarna.* 2 vols. Leiden: Brill.

———. 2017. "Death and the Sun Temple: New Evidence for Private Mortuary Cults at Amarna." *JEA* 103: 117–23.

Winckler, H. 1896. *Die Thontafeln von Tell-el-Amarna.* Berlin: Reuther & Reichard.

Worms, M. 1916. "Nefretiti." *Journal asiatique* sér. 11, 7: 469–91.

Wong, L., S. Rickerby, A. Phenix, A. Rava, and R. Kamal. 2012. "Examination of the Wall Paintings in Tutankhamen's Tomb: Inconsistencies in Original Technology." In *The Decorative: Conservation and the Applied Arts: Contributions to the 2012 IIC Congress Preprints, Vienna,* S322–30. London: International Institute for Conservation of Historic and Artistic Works.

Woolley, C.L. 1922. "Excavations at Tell el-Amarna." *JEA* 8: 48–82.

Zivie, C.M. 1976. *Giza au deuxième millénaire.* Cairo: Institut français d'archéologie orientale.

SOURCES OF IMAGES

All images by author unless otherwise noted.

5a. Davies 1941: pl. 29–30.

5b. Epigraphic Survey 1980: pl. 9.

9. Centre franco-égyptien d'étude des Temples de Karnak.

11. Metropolitan Museum of Art.

12. Redford 1984: figs. 6–7; 1973: pl. vii.

13. Redford 1975: pl. vb.

17. Davies 1903–1908: pl. iv.

19. Smith 1912: pl. xcix.

24. Davies 1941: pl. 33–36.

27. Davies 1903–1908: V: pl. xxxvii.

29. Dyan Hilton/Whittemore 1926: pl. ii.

30. after Kemp 1995: figs. 15.14.

32. Dyan Hilton.

44. Davies 1903–1908: vi, xxix–xxx.

45. Jan Koek.

47. restoration: Davies 1923: 42, fig. 4.

50. Roeder 1969: pl. 105[56-VIIIA], 106[831-VIIIA].

52. Roeder 1969: pl.21[454-VI].

54. Metropolitan Museum of Art.

55, bottom. Brooklyn Museum.

59. Dyan Hilton.

61. Trustees of the British Museum.

67. Davies 1903–1908: III, pl. xiii–xv; II, pl. xxxvii.

71. Martin 1989: pl. 63.

73, top. Roeder 1969: [783-VIIIA+794-VIIIA]

73, bottom. Metropolitan Museum of Art.

74. adapted from Davies 1903–1908: II, pl. xxvii, xxxvii, xli; Lepsius 1849–59: pl. 99a; 1897: 2:138; Moseley 2009: 144, fig. 7.8.
75. adapted from Nicholson 1870: pl. 1[4].
76, left. Harry Burton.
76, right. D.J. Kidd (Harrison 1966: pl. xxviii[1]).
80. Athena Van der Perre.
81. photo: Harry Burton.
84, top. Roeder 1969: pl. 10[826-VIIIA].
85. Roeder 1969: pl. 6[777-VIIIC], 16[406-VIIA].
87. photo: National Museums Liverpool (World Museum).
89. adapted from Kemp and Stevens 2010: 117 fig. 2.16 and Kemp 2016: 15.
90. photos: Petrie Museum and Pendlebury 1951: pl. lxxiii[8]; drawing: adapted from Stewart 1976: pl. 12 and Allen 1988: 118, fig. 1.
91. facsimile from Gardiner 1928: pl. v–vi.
97. Erman 1900: 113.
100. North Sinai Archaeological Project.
101, left. Dyan Hilton.
102, right. Brooklyn Museum.
104. Robert Partridge.
110. adapted from Theban Mapping Project.
111. Stephen Cross.
113. Victor Loret.
116. archival photograph.
118. Prisse d'Avennes 1847: pl. xi.
119. adapted from Petrie 1894: pl xv.
120. adapted from Kemp and Garfi 1993.
124. Prince Johann Georg of Saxony.
126. archive photograph.
130, left. El-Zeft.

INDEX

Names of rulers of Egypt are given in CAPITALS.

Alphanumerics in parentheses are those of an individual's tomb and/or house.